DEFENDING ACCESS

A CRITIQUE OF STANDARDS
IN HIGHER EDUCATION

TOM FOX

Boynton/Cook Publishers
HEINEMANN
PORTSMOUTH, NH

For Jean, Nicky, Louise, and Joey

Boynton/Cook Publishers, Inc.
A subsidiary of Reed Elsevier Inc.
361 Hanover Street
Portsmouth, NH 03801–3912
http://www.boyntoncook.com

Offices and agents throughout the world

The author and publisher wish to thank those who have generously given permission to reprint borrowed material:

Portions of "The Backlash Against Access" originally appeared as "Standards and Access" in *Journal of Basic Writing,* Spring 1993, Volume 12, Number 1. Copyright © 1993 by the Journal of Basic Writing, Instructional Resource Center, Office of Academic Affairs, The City University of New York. Used by permission of the Editors.

Portions of "The Dialectic of Standards and Access in Nineteenth-Century Writing Instruction" originally appeared as "From Freedom to Manners: African American Literacy in the Nineteenth Century" in *Composition Forum,* Winter 1995, Volume 6, Number 1. Used by permission of the Editor.

Portions of "Ideologies of Access and Exclusion: Basic Writing and Cultural Conflict" originally appeared as "Basic Writing as Cultural Conflict" in *Journal of Education,* 1990, Volume 172, Number 1. Used by permission of the Trustees of Boston University.

Library of Congress Cataloging-in-Publication Data
Fox, Tom.
    Defending access : a critique of standards in higher education / Tom Fox.
      p. cm.
    Includes bibliographical references and index.
    ISBN 0-86709-461-3 (alk. paper)
    1. Universities and colleges—United States—Admission. 2. Education, Higher—Standards—United States. 3. Minorities—Education (Higher)—United States.
4. Educational equalization—United States. 5. Affirmative action programs—United States. I. Title.
LB2351.2.F688 1999
378.1'61'0973—dc21
                              98-53405
                                CIP

Editor: Lisa Luedeke
Production: Elizabeth Valway
Cover design: Jenny Jensen Greenleaf
Manufacturing: Louise Richardson

Printed in the United States of America on acid-free paper
Docutech T & C 2007

Contents

Preface

Standards are the talk of the day, from the National Council of Teachers of English (NCTE) to English Department mailrooms. Some of the talk is progressive: Teachers are thinking of ways to challenge students to achieve more, to be more thoughtful and reflective about their writing, to be more effective and powerful in their critiques, to turn their attention to compelling and important topics to write about. These are the standards that I argue for in this book. They are context-specific, dealing with the students and curriculum at particular institutions in particular communities. Sometimes, the best talk about standards is even student-specific, exploring with other teachers in the hallways or during the morning commute the ways that Amy can research more deeply, or Janeen can see the need to reach a broader audience, or Rob can critique his conclusions instead of just defending them. These standards grow from teachers of writing who are aware of the new ambitions for the teaching of writing that composition studies has set for itself in the past two decades of professional work.

The standards talk has also been unproductive. Uninformed commentary about the supposed declining literacy of college students continues to be played out in endless versions of "Why Johnny Can't Write" in both popular media and in everyday conversations among professors, teachers, and parents, despite the absence of real historical evidence. Often these refrains of falling standards implicitly or explicitly refer to immigrant students or students of color whose difference—cultural and/or linguistic—is more at issue than their performance. These complaints, among others, have produced calls for state and national standards in literacy. While some discussions of these standards may have helped teachers revise their sense of teaching practices, the resulting standards documents, I argue, are liable to do as much harm as good. This book critiques the seemingly automatic move to acontextual standards each time new groups of students press for access.

Defending Access is arranged in two parts. Chapters 1–3 build a critique of standards in higher education by demonstrating how they have been—and still are—used less as a way of raising expectations for students than as a means of excluding students new to higher education. Chapter 1 examines contemporary uses of standards in higher education and challenges the relationship between language standards and access. Chapters 2 and 3 work from the framework of concerns outlined in the first chapter to explore the ways that the history of standards and access in higher education have exerted force on the ways we have shaped our curriculum and pedagogy. The last two chapters examine ways of working for access in writing-program administration and pedagogy.

Throughout *Defending Access* I focus on African American students and their writing. Though I believe virtually none of my argument is exclusively relevant to African American students, I am also convinced that mainstream American society and the educational establishment consistently ignore the ways that school has not worked well for many African Americans. We suffer from a destructive forgetfulness. While an event such as the Los Angeles riots may provoke a storm of concern for the state of urban education and the broken promises of justice, this storm is a summer shower: briefly drenching the soil, but not ending the drought.

Acknowledgments

As a teacher and a writer, I have tried to listen carefully to both African American scholars in composition and especially to African American students. I have been rewarded by these students through their excellent academic work and by more trust than I could reasonably expect, given the current state of race relations. While relationships between white teachers and black students have to overcome a history of mistrust, I have never found students unwilling to try. I would like to thank them collectively here for sharing their trust and their work with me. I owe special thanks to my research assistant and former student, Aaron Oforlea, for his insights into white perspectives on African American education, for his trust, humor, and persistence.

Parts of this book have been previously published, though all have been revised for this book. Parts of Chapter 1 first appeared in the *Journal of Basic Writing;* parts of Chapter 2 first appeared in *Composition Forum;* parts of Chapter 3 first appeared in the *Journal of Education.* My thanks to all of these journals for permission to reprint this material.

Additionally, several scholars in composition have been extraordinarily helpful. Foremost are my colleagues at California State University, Chico: Judith Rodby and Thia Wolf. Their intelligence, generosity, and hard, good work made this book possible. My deepest thanks. David Bleich has consistently supported my work for nearly fifteen years. He has contributed his insights, suggested sources, and talked about the issues of this book with concern and thoughtfulness. Many other scholars in composition studies have made contributions, reading parts or even the entire manuscript; among them, Marilyn Cooper, Diana George, Joe Harris, Bruce Horner, Min-Zhan Lu, and Gary Olson. I wish to make clear that "contribution" does not necessarily entail "agreement." Particularly, since I write about the relationships between the administration and the writing program on my own campus in Chapter 4, I want to make clear that my interpretation of the events and documents does not necessarily represent the views of the other writing faculty at California State University, Chico.

I received a California State University Research Grant to draft one version of the manuscript. I thank the university and my colleagues for making it possible to write at a time of decreasing support for faculty.

Chapter One

The Backlash Against Access

In the last twenty years various groups of people—African American, Latino, women, gay and lesbian, Asian American, among others—have fought for increased access to higher education. Many of these groups linked this struggle with social and political movements, such as the continuing battle for civil rights for African Americans, the struggle for safe and productive lives for women, arguments for the acceptance and support of gay and lesbian people, and the fight for legitimacy and respect for those who speak languages and dialects other than standard English. These political struggles are represented in higher education by arguments over what constitutes canons in various disciplines, in discussions about the various forms and amounts of writing assessment, in controversies over proposed policies concerning racial and sexual harassment, and in debates over affirmative-action policies for admission and hiring. These issues have received a great deal of attention in both professional journals and popular newspapers, weekly news magazines, and even on television. Less obviously, but perhaps more importantly, the challenge to make higher education more inclusive has affected talk in the mailroom, commentary on students' papers, faculty morale, hiring practices, and all the day-to-day work that people who work in English Departments and composition programs do. Central to all these discussions, yet often assumed or indirectly stated, is the issue of standards. Without much consideration, and with little conscious criticism, questions of access become questions of standards.

This book argues that, despite the pressure from political groups, lack of access remains our most crucial problem. If higher education is going to serve democratic purposes, that is, if higher education is going to be a means of redistributing wealth and privilege to people of color, women, and other marginalized groups, then increased access is

1

the critical first step. Standards, however, often inhibit access. This has been true historically, as Chapters 2 and 3 demonstrate, and is true today as standards emerge as a central educational topic at the same time anti-affirmative action, anti-immigrant, and English Only legislation are enacted. My argument is not a causal one, but one that recognizes the co-emergence of two issues, the pressure for access and the attention to standards. In the swirl of cultural concerns, these two issues are now, as they have been in the past, in a dialectical relationship.

Of course the question of access is far from settled. Despite all the controversy surrounding multiculturalism, affirmative action, and the supposedly changing canon, we see no great change in the racial or ethnic makeup of students or faculty in four-year colleges and universities. We see little change in the ways that writing is assessed despite persuasive arguments against both multiple-choice tests and one-shot timed tests. We see surprisingly little change in the actual texts chosen in literature classes, despite exaggerated reports claiming that Alice Walker is replacing Shakespeare. Yet the backlash against these supposed changes in higher education seems to be growing stronger. And central to the arguments of those resisting access are claims that literary, pedagogical, and scholarly standards are lowered as a consequence of increased access.

Exploring the Backlash

I would like to begin this chapter by looking at the conservative arguments concerning standards and access. The wish for a homogeneous past is a subtle but persistent theme in right-wing criticisms of higher education. Take, for instance the following three quotations concerning standards in higher education. These points of view represent the current cultural ground, the points of view that dominate discussions about standards. I will be discussing texts by Dinesh D'Souza, William Bennett, and Allan Bloom, but many other commentators share these points of view.

The first quotation is from William Bennett's book *The Devaluing of America: The Fight for Our Culture and Our Children:*

> Since the late 1960's, there has been a collective loss of nerve and faith on the part of many faculty and academic administrators. The academy has hurt itself, even disgraced itself, in many ways. Course requirements were thrown out; intellectual authority was relinquished; standards were swept aside; scholarship increasingly became an extension of political activism; and many colleges and universities lost a clear sense of their educational mission and their conception of what a graduate of their institution ought to know or be. (1992, 156)

Next is Dinesh D'Souza, from *Illiberal Education: The Politics of Race and Sex on Campus:*

> Standards of merit will always, and should be, debated to discover how well they measure the skills that are sought. This debate, however, has nothing to do with whether groups end up overrepresented or under-represented, because the standards measure not group but individual performance. One can only raise the statistical average of a group by improving the achievement of the individuals within it. (1991, 189)

Finally, here's Allan Bloom, from *The Closing of the American Mind:*

> Affirmative action now institutionalizes the worst aspect of separatism. The fact is that the average black student's achievements do not equal those of the average white student in the good universities, and every-body knows it. It is also a fact that the university degree of a black student is also tainted, and employers look on it with suspicion, or be-come guilty accomplices in the toleration of incompetence. (1987, 96)

Those of us schooled in postmodernism and supportive of affirmative action and multiculturalism may be tempted to ignore such statements as hopelessly misinformed, naive, and wrongheaded. Yet simply dis-missing or mocking these authors misses the opportunity to examine the ways we may be unwittingly complicit in their arguments. Through-out this book, I argue that unless we rigorously examine the assump-tions about standards that we hold, our political commitment to eco-nomic and social access for students is compromised.

I'll begin by examining the assumptions upon which these claims about standards rest. Look at Bennett's list of the accomplishments of the late 1960s first: "Course requirements were thrown out; intellec-tual authority was relinquished; standards were swept aside; . . ." Ray-mond Williams' gloss on standards in *Keywords* helps illuminate Ben-nett's understanding of the use of standards. By distinguishing between singular and ordinary plurals, Williams explains why "standards" has become predominantly a term associated with those who wish to con-serve and maintain institutions and language. He defines the "plural singular" sense of the word *standards* as

> essentially CONSENSUAL (q.v.) ("we all know what real standards are") or, with a certain deliberate vagueness, suasive ("anyone who is concerned with standards will agree"). It is often impossible, in these uses, to disagree with some assertion of **standards** without appearing to disagree with the very idea of quality; this is where the singular plural most powerfully operates. (1983, 297)

In the plural singular sense of the word, standards are like morals or values, you either have them or you don't. When used in a phrase like "university standards," Williams argues, the word refers to "generalized version of the essence of a . . . university being projected as if it were a specific grouping of . . . **standardizations**" (1983, 298). This plural singular sense of standards seeks essence, not contexts, seeks objectivity, not values that are contingent upon historical or material needs. Note that Bennett is using the word "standards," a plural, as if it were singular. So when Bennett says "standards were swept aside," he counts on a consensual agreement; standards are not named, "we all know" what they are. He also endorses a singular idea of standards, much like the way that "family values" was used by the Republican party in the 1992 presidential campaign: You either have them—and that's good; or you don't—and that's bad. And by doing so, he limits the response to either agreement or disagreement.

This rhetorical strategy indicates a deep ideological difference between Bennett and those of us in the academy who understand standards as more of an ordinary plural. For all the references to students' lack of history in Bennett's discourse, his own view of standards is profoundly ahistorical. These are free-floating standards, not explicitly rooted in any historical need or condition. The most powerful rejoinder to Bennett's claim that "standards were swept aside" is to reject his either/or claim for the word and attempt to point out the ways in which Bennett's standards (the ones swept aside in the sixties) far from being transcendent or objective are, like everyone else's, *contingent*. I use the term from Barbara Herrnstein Smith's book, *Contingency of Values*, which makes the case that all evaluations are dependent on and related to historical and social conditions. The use of standards in this quotation by Bennett works to uphold the *conditions* of the pre-1960s university, without really stating what those conditions were. It also denies the existence and relevance of claims that these conditions were unjust.

Let's move now to the second quotation. In this statement, D'Souza seems to be indicating that standards aren't automatic or assumed: "Standards of merit will always, and should be, debated to discuss how well they measure the skills that are sought." He seems here to be granting us the point that standards may change, that they are, in some sense, "contingent." However, he also asserts that the contingencies are not social or historical, but only individual. It takes just a moment of reflection to realize that his point amounts to a non sequitur. Standards are by definition a social agreement (i.e., Williams' point that standards are "consensual"); that's why they can be debated. Yet D'Souza denies this social contract by saying that standards are set socially but measure only individual achievement. While it is true that individuals take tests, this is hardly a startling observation. The next step, is startling, however: Because we take tests individually, group measurement is irrelevant. We ought to reflect a moment on the bizarre nature of this claim; it would mean, for instance, that the disparity on standardized tests between African Americans and white students is the result of coincidence.

Behind D'Souza's claim is a web of values that inhibits collectivity, that seeks to deflate the strength of social identification, that prevents oppressed groups from seeing their situations as the result of systemic injustice, not individual failure. We have moved from Bennett's claims of objectivity to D'Souza's claim of individualism. The two discourses have in common the ability to obscure "contingencies" or render competing contingencies irrelevant and nonexistent (Smith 1988, 41).

Neither Bennett nor D'Souza says exactly what contingencies their laments about standards are based on, and that's part of their argument. Allan Bloom doesn't either, but his statements on race, which are echoed by Bennett and D'Souza, give us a glimpse into what's going on here. Let's start with the most offensive passage: "The fact is that the average black student's achievements do not equal those of the average white student in the good universities, and everybody knows it." This quotation moves from objective and irrefutable standards (as indicated by the quotation "everybody knows it") to the rejection of institutional and curricular changes that invite participation and success to students of color. All of the authors I have cited make this same move; their critique of falling or abandoned standards is always accompanied by a critique of affirmative action and multiculturalism.

The arguments that connect standards with multiculturalism reveal the contingencies under which these authors make claims about standards. Each author claims to be reasserting a standard that supposedly existed in the past and is now threatened or abandoned, without dealing with students whose diverse histories and cultures challenge an easy comparison. This wish for the mythic equal past leads to some wild claims about the present. Bloom asserts, erroneously, that "[t]here is now a large black presence in major universities, frequently equivalent to their proportion in the general population" (1987, 91); Bennett asserts, unbelievably, that "[w]e have basically overcome the legacy of slavery" (1992, 189). These assertions, nevertheless, finally explain what all the fuss is about. Bennett, Bloom, and D'Souza say outright that they wish to return to a university ideology that predates both postmodernism and the attempted, but still largely unsuccessful, integration of the university. They claim that their version of the university will provide students of color with academic and economic access, even though history has proved them wrong. And they then assert that multicultural education and affirmative action actually deny access.

It should not surprise us that arguments about access should emerge in these discussions of standards. It's familiar; students' access to academic and economic privilege is contingent upon meeting standards.

Many of us ascribe to a similar contingency when we seek to empower our students by giving them either the language of the academy or the language of the dominant culture. This is inviting; it gives our classrooms and our profession a sense of action and power, a sense that we are making a difference in our students' lives. But we fall into the trap of imagining that language standards and social boundaries are one and the same. If we tell ourselves and our students that they will achieve access if they master writing standards, we are obscuring and underestimating the powerful forces of racism, sexism, elitism, and heterosexism that continue to operate despite the students' mastery of standards.

The Problem in Higher Education

Conservative critics have singled out higher education as institutions that have sacrificed quality for access. However, higher education has lagged behind other segments of education in providing access somewhat resembling the ethnic makeup of the United States. Consider that high school graduation rates for students of color (especially African American and Latino) have risen in the last ten years and have narrowed the gap between students of color and white students. For those who doubt that this figure represents real achievement, there are also corresponding improvements in SAT scores. Since 1976, for instance, scores for African American students have risen twenty-four points in the verbal segment and thirty-four points in math. This is all the more impressive considering that twice as many minority students took the test in 1995 as in 1974 (National Center for Educational Statistics, 1996). This improvement should translate into more students of color interested in, applying for, and entering four-year universities. But it doesn't. In fact, the percentage of entering minority freshman in four-year universities, especially for African Americans, has remained about the same during the 1980s (between 27 and 30 percent for African Americans) and has only recently risen somewhat during the 1990s to about 35 percent. The gap between white enrollment and black enrollment has grown from a difference of 4.5 percent to a difference of 8.1 percent in 1994 (Smith 1996). African Americans, although attending higher education in slightly greater numbers than ten years ago, are losing comparative ground to white students.

There has been little public outcry about this gap and virtually no media attention has been focused on this gap in access. Instead, the public's attention has been drawn to a series of voter initiatives and legal efforts that would further reduce access. For instance, access was directly limited by a voter initiative in California in 1994, Proposition 187, which made various sorts of government services out-of-bounds for undocumented immigrants. The "Save Our State" committee, which bankrolled and campaigned for this initiative, included in Proposition 187 two sections that singled out education—Sections 7 and 8, titled "Exclusion of Illegal Aliens from Public Elementary and Secondary Schools" and "Exclusion of Illegal Aliens from Public Postsecondary Educational Institutions." These sections specifically exclude undocumented immigrants from schooling. Additionally, it means that all people who look like they might be undocumented immigrants (those with brown skin or Asian features for example) come under suspicion. It was overwhelmingly approved by voters in California.

A year later, the Board of Regents of the University of California (UC), decided to end affirmative-action programs for women and people of color, effective 1997. The UC regents claimed—without any significant evidence and against the claims of faculty at UC Berkeley who actually have contact with students—that the admission policies lowered quality, lowered standards. Only a very small percentage of students are admitted using different standards. To be accepted at the University of California campuses, students must rank in the top twelve and one-half percent of their high school graduating class, except for 5 percent of incoming students who are classified as "disadvantaged" by race, gender, or poverty or an exceptional ability that would argue for their acceptance (Wallace 1995, A30). In 1994, only 698 students were admitted through the "disadvantaged" category *systemwide* (nine campuses). Not all of these were admitted because of race. Given the minute numbers here, spread out over nine large university campuses, it strains credibility to imagine that these few students lower standards.

As with the example of the literary canon cited earlier, the backlash against access exceeds the actual numbers. Despite the truly paltry numbers of students admitted under affirmative action, the regents decided that affirmative action was damaging standards. This indicates that their move was about limiting the use of higher education to create a democratic society rather than about any actual case of lowering standards. This use of standards, as a means to protect the status quo, has historical precedents; we know each time standards are called into question, each time professors or educational bureaucrats begin to moan about the falling quality of student work, what's really underfoot is a desire to make sure the same students who have always gone to college still go.

A spin-off of the UC decision is the misnamed California Civil Rights Initiative (CCRI). The arguments for the CCRI work on three levels. The first is on principle: Discrimination is wrong, affirmative action discriminates against whites, therefore affirmative action is wrong. The second is that since people of color are given "privilege" by affirmative action, their achievements are suspect. The third is on standards:

Affirmative action lowers standards for people of color and therefore lowers standards for the institution.

It is tempting to rehearse the arguments for affirmative action, but for this book, the important point to acknowledge is that when access threatens change, standards are always one of the tools used to resist that change. These standards are almost always based on the measurement of abilities by "standardized" tests such as the LSAT, SAT, GRE, or by grade point average.

The various movements to limit access show no signs of stopping. California's English Only law is poised to become a national law; several states are considering versions of the CCRI. A new proposition eliminating bilingual education has been passed in California, and anti-immigrant fever has taken hold even in places where immigrants are few. What is terrifying about the change from the 1980s to the 1990s is that during the 1980s, anti-multicultural arguments focused on curriculum and texts. The 1990s backlash seems aimed directly at people and their relationship with institutions. The anti-affirmative action initiative, English Only, and Proposition 187 seek to reverse minute, almost imaginary changes toward a multicultural society. The result is policies that will keep students of color out of higher education and, nearly as damaging, confirm many students' fears that educational institutions really don't want them anyway.

NCTE Standards Project

The political climate in California mirrored the national mood toward education, even in the relatively liberal Clinton administration. Worried about the repeated cries of crises in education, the federal government proposed "national standards" in a number of content areas as a way to insure that teachers and students toe the line. In 1992, the National Council of Teachers of English (NCTE), a professional organization representing English teachers at all levels, entered into a partnership with the International Reading Association, the Center for the Study of Reading, and the federal government to produce national standards in English. They sought to include teachers at all levels and at every step of the way. They also sought to enter actively into the standards/access cultural battle by arguing for standards that also require resources to achieve them. NCTE's main arguments for standards are that teachers will benefit from having enlightened national standards behind them, that they "will recognize their students, themselves, their goals, and their daily endeavors in this document; so too, they will be inspired, motivated, and provoked to reevaluate some of what they do in class. By engaging with these standards, teachers, will, we hope, also think and talk energetically about the assumptions that underlie their own classroom practices and those of their colleagues" (NCTE 1996, 24).

This statement positions standards in dialectical relationships with teachers; they are created by teachers in order to improve teaching. In this sense they are laudable and carry on the traditions of teacher respect and professionalism historically encouraged by NCTE. In fact, NCTE's insistence on the involvement of teachers was one of the reasons that in March of 1994 the federal government withdrew its support of the project, although there were other reasons as well. The government's withdrawal was also a signal that the NCTE's standards might not easily support the traditional kind of cultural work that national standards are meant to do: limit access. NCTE has emphasized that their standards are meant to support good teachers and serve to increase access for students from all backgrounds. NCTE and IRA completed the standards document and it is now one of NCTE's best-selling books.

The problem, however, is that NCTE's good intentions and democratic process do not in themselves create a standards document that will work for access. The working contexts of many teachers do not support a collective and thoughtful examination of standards. Instead, teachers often feel unsupported and see standards as another threat to their autonomy. It would be easy for an administrator or a school board to turn the standards into a remedial tool and threaten the teachers with compliance. Of course, NCTE and the standards document oppose such use of the standards. But when standards historically have been used for just such purposes, then the document, however framed, will, in many cases, conform to its historic use. Lil Brannon, in "The Problem of National Standards," argues that the standards document will play into the hands of those who wish to restrict teachers' intellectual freedom and professionalism: "Standards, even those we agree with, even those that are constructed with good intentions, can and do turn into repressive dogma" (1995, 445).

Miles Myers, Executive Director of NCTE, is insightful about the nature of standards and their relationship with access. His argument for national standards rests on a historical examination of legal decisions about equity. He argues that equity issues in education, especially in the legal arena, have shifted from questions of access to questions of adequacy. Early decisions about equality in education, such as *Brown vs. Topeka*, "established the principle of open access to and equal funding of schools" (1995, 438). Therefore, Myers says, the experts needed for testimony were "demographers, managers of bus schedules, and experts on the U.S. census" (439). In contrast, the new cases of inequality in schooling will, he believes, be argued on whether or not the curriculum content is adequate. In such cases, equality would be determined not just by access, but by a high-quality curriculum and high-achieving students, what Myers calls "adequacy." In these cases, the expert witnesses would be writing instructors. To back up their case and to give it a national punch, these new experts would need to refer to some kind of "documentation of adequacy" (439), at which point the national standards would become crucial.

As compelling as Myers' argument is, it underestimates the power of social and institutional contexts to shape the use of the standards. At no time in history has a movement for national standards been fought for by the powerless. Historically, calls for standards, as John Trimbur suggests in "Literacy and the Discourse of Crisis," have not be prompted by failures of instruction or achievement, but by antidemocratic ideological and political forces (Trimbur 1991, 294). The NCTE document will have to work against the expectations that standards have been historically used to maintain social hierarchies; it will have to play on the public media field dominated by conservative critics of education. The standards document, I fear, will either provide grist for the conservative media's mill, languish on administrators' shelves, or be turned against good teachers. It will not, I believe, improve the lives of teachers as they fight for access and challenge their students.

Standards for Teachers Versus Teachers' Standards

My text, too, has great potential to be grist for conservative critics' mill, because by arguing against national standards, it appears to be arguing against quality, excellence, or rigor. It is impossible to teach without standards, and teaching without challenging standards is usually bad teaching. The distinction I wish to make is between the standards that a teacher holds as provisional goals for his or her students, which develop out of and are modified by interactions in context, and bureaucratic standards that almost always emerge from a political context of crisis. Historically, these bureaucratic standards have been used against teachers and against access.

My argument is that there is not a crisis of standards, but a continuing crisis of access. This crisis of access is caused by wide-ranging economic, social, and political issues—only some of which can be solved by changes in higher education. I want to argue specifically and strongly against the narrow view that the crisis of access is caused mainly by underpreparation or a lack of literacy skills on the part of students of color.

Yet the narrow view, that lack of access is caused by lack of skills, is powerful and dominant in both the public's and the profession's minds. Most remedial programs are set up to provide access by remediating skills. Most equal opportunity programs seek ways to bolster students' skills as a means of retention (more sophisticated programs also provide contexts for students to reflect on the conflicts and continuities of home and university life).

In my experience as a teacher, however, the lack of skills only rarely explains failure. Instead, failure is usually caused by a complex web of social and political circumstances. These circumstances are hardly ever experienced or perceived as "political," but instead are cast as individual maturity problems, lack of organization, intellectual deficits, psychological problems, lack of preparation, and other individual faults of students. On my campus—and, if media reports are at all reliable, on other campuses, too—these "failures" are held up as examples of lowered standards and excess access. But the stories of access—and failed access—involve complicated and recalcitrant political problems.

What follows are three short narratives of students who failed or almost failed. By telling these stories, I hope to remind teachers of writing of the students who didn't show up for class or who handed papers in late or who disappeared suddenly. So far I have mapped out the territory of this book in general terms; the student examples extend my argument in more concrete ways, showing how the material realities of American society affect student performance.

Alice's Story: "I want to hold reality in my hand."

I begin with a student paper. The author, Alice, is African American. This paper was written in response to the chapter in Malcolm X's autobiography ("Saved") where he teaches himself to read and write. She was enrolled—by virtue of a placement test—in a basic writing course that asked students to examine their own language-learning histories. This is her first draft:

> The prison I have is my own fault. It deals with me pressuring myself to succeed in life, because I don't want the problems of being unable to do what I want to do and when I want to do. If I didn't think negative of myself not being able to succeed in life, because of the pressure I put on myself, then life would not be such a headache. I'm coming to the problem where I really don't know my captivity, it could be me, trying to get myself ahead in life without having the patients I need to really get ahead in life. If I didn't go through the problem of bewildering myself then maybe it wouldn't be so rough for me, to be patient and wait for the future ahead. But know not me I see such a bright future for myself that I don't know how to pase myself in waiting for it. I picture in my mind everyday on how I see my future. It's good, but I'm tired of dreaming, thats all, I'm just tired, and I want reality in my hands right now. . . . So far all my dreams up to this point of me succeeding to the level that I want to achieve to has happened, but I still

have a long ways to go. I'm out of high school now and time in college is my parents money. And I can't waste time with their money. So I keep myself busy so I don't waste their time and mine. I found out what my captivity is, its' me trying to satisfy my parents, by going over the limits of what the college education is for, and thats me. Now I feel a lot better, I'm really going to college for me and thats really what its all about. It was my choice to come here not theirs. Because I'm the one doing the work and not them, I'm struggling to do what I have been dreaming of for a long time, its my turn to prove to myself what I can achieve in life with the time that I have. So I don't feel trapped any more. This is the captivity that I am experienceing now. So I can help myself get away from it since it's on the surface to my knowledge. What's set me free in writing is this assignment. Reason why, is, because I have told my feelings of the problem on paper so it's free from my mind and my head doesn't hurt as bad as it has in the past semester and up to this point now.

I was in my second semester of full-time teaching when Alice wrote this paper. I duplicated her work for the class (which was a regular practice) and asked students to appreciate the complex issues that Alice was writing about: the conflict between dreams and reality, the conflict between education and home life, and the honest difficulty of knowing how to handle what Alice calls "the real world." I told her I liked her piece very much, too, and that it belonged, with revisions and editing, in her portfolio due at the end of the semester. In the class as a whole, and in conference, I began the discussion of these issues with the hope of helping Alice turn this piece into a critique. I told her I would help her edit her piece. Alice was absent then for several class meetings. When she returned we talked and she referred vaguely to problems at home and brought her revised piece. It still needed editing. Her major change was this final paragraph:

> There's a new turn for me and my future. I'm going to think more positive and not negative, because thinking negative isn't going to get me anywhere. My dreams are going to come true if thats the last thing I do. I'm going all the way to make my life fulfilled with all sorts of excitments, because I feel I deserve it. I'm working long and hard to find happiness, until I do I still won't be satisfied. I'll be out looking for more excitment to keep me happy. I need to be happy with my life if I want to live. Without happiness whats the use of me living. I can't live with the facted of me being unhappy for the rest of my life. I know of the hard times that are going to come, but when they come I will handle them then, but while I'm young I'm going to live it to the fullness. There maybe times where I might feel down, but I have to pick myself back up and just start again.
>
> Life isn't ment to waste and I'm surely not going to waste my life.

She missed the next two weeks, and I decided that she couldn't pass the class with that many absences. She returned with the third draft of this paper (which was retyped but otherwise unchanged), and most of her other portfolio pieces. I decided I had to stick to my policy and tell her that I couldn't pass her because she had missed more than one quarter of the class meetings. When I think about this meeting, the look on Alice's face stands out. She was not surprised or angry, but quietly accepting. This news hit her with all the surprise of the inevitable first frost of winter. And then she told me that she was probably going to drop out of school entirely and that she was having problems in the rest of her classes, too.

Alice was not the first student that I have failed, nor the first African American that I have failed. I don't think I handled Alice's situation terribly or insensitively.

I would like to use Alice's paper as a way of exploring the issues raised by this book, beginning with the first sentence: "The prison I have is my own fault." The term "prison" is an artifact of the assignment—a response to Malcolm X—but her use of it is interesting. Alice presents "prison" as a psychological state that comes from the lack of correspondence between her dreams and reality. The reasoning behind her first sentence is that because it is a "psychological" state, it must be up to her to change her outlook. The remarkable revision results from this psychological stance. She asserts, as if writing itself was proof, that she will think positively and not negatively and that this is cause for "a new turn for me and my future." At the same time, lurking within this positive and hopeful vision is a lingering sense of despair, a commentary on her dismal present: "I need to be happy with my life if I want to live. Without happiness whats the use of me living. I can't live with the facted of me being unhappy for the rest of my life."

Alice's prison is staged (and probably experienced) as a psychological drama between depression and hope. It is individually experienced, and "freedom" (which transmogrifies rather subtly into "happiness") is won by a change of attitude. This is the way most of us think, an artifact of both traditional American individualism and Norman Vincent Peale psychologism.

In a minor key, what Houston Baker's *Blues, Ideology, and Afro-American Literature* calls the *sotto voce*, is a more material perspective: "I'm out of high school now and time in college is my parents money." With this realization, however, Alice returns to the psychological perspective; in effect, it's the talking cure, once she has stated what the problem is, she says, "So I don't feel trapped anymore." People do feel this way, and I won't underestimate the power of naming a problem, but naming the problem on the paper doesn't solve the problem in day-to-day life. Despite this, she writes: "What's set me free in writing is this assignment." Whenever students write something like this, I am suspicious, although in Alice's case, the suspicion is not that she wants a good grade. We had talked in class about the different uses of writing, the ways that it can be put to use for freedom. One student spoke of how she used writing to break up with her boyfriend because she could never win a verbal argument; other students discussed the ways that writing helped them to understand a problem and then act on it (which is close to Alice's statement here). But no essay, whether grounded in psychological or material perceptions of reality, would have relieved the pressure that Alice felt. Although the real reasons for Alice's dropping out were never fully disclosed to me, urgencies of time and money were central. One thing was clear: Her failure was not due to a lack of skills in writing. Yes, she needed work on several levels, but I have no doubt she could do it.

Greg: The Basics Revisited

At a recent department retreat on pedagogy, a colleague of mine suggested that we (the composition faculty) "quit trying to save the world and just teach writing instead." Putting aside his exaggeration of "save the world," I argued that politics and pedagogy are not only theoretically related, but also related in the experience of individual students. This integration of politics and pedagogy has, in the past few years of composition studies, come close to being a meaningless mantra, but I seek to recover the meaning from abstraction by looking carefully at daily lives of writing teachers, administrators, and writing students. Consider Greg, for instance, one of two students in my composition class last semester who was in danger of failing. Greg wrote reasonably well, certainly well enough to pass the course, but began to miss classes. When I asked why, he said it was a problem of housing. I pressed and found out that he had "lost" his housing and was living with friends off campus. On Thursdays (it was a Tuesday-Thursday class) he said he had difficulties getting a ride to campus for my class. I helped him work it out with a classmate and, for a time, his attendance improved. He also wrote an excellent piece, far more sophisticated and polished than his earlier works, on a series of racist incidents in Chico, including the burning of a house that was used as an adjunct to his fraternity. This incident had not been reported in either the city newspaper or the college newspaper as a racist incident, although Greg wrote that it clearly was. I encouraged him to send it to the campus newspaper.

He began to miss classes again. This time two weeks straight. I felt, at this point, that he would fail the class. I left messages at his home, and waited. During my office hours, Greg finally showed up. He looked depressed. I noticed his jeans were dirty. "What's going on, Greg?" He told me it was still a problem with housing. He told me that he had been trying to stay with different friends, that his financial aid had been canceled, then reinstated, but he wouldn't get his check for several weeks. He said he was going to quit. Then he told me that the last friend that he stayed with, when he shook his hand good-bye one morning, had slipped him a twenty dollar bill. Greg said he couldn't go back. And he said he was ashamed. I asked where he had been staying and he answered, "Around." "Greg," I said, "have you been sleeping outside?" He nodded.

That day he got his financial aid, and with university help, he got housing. But the whole scene haunted me. I have hesitated to write about it, worried that I would tell a tearjerker, a maudlin tale. But it's true and I think it's true more often than anyone wants to know. It makes me think about the absurdity of asking for "typewritten" papers (Greg had been using the library's computer and printer), and the difficulty of concentrating on writing assignments when food, shelter, and safety are at risk. I was reminded of a remarkable moment in Denny Taylor and Catherine Dorsey-Gaines' *Growing up Literate*. After several chapters that not only describe the wide-ranging literate activities of the families on Shay Avenue, but also describe the unending struggle for housing, food, and safety, Taylor and Dorsey-Gaines break the master narrative of ethnography and suddenly question their whole enterprise:

> There was a time early in the study that we found it hard to justify our literacy research. With these families struggling to provide food and shelter for their children, why were we studying their reading and writing? What was the point? How could a study of literacy help them? It was difficult for us to think that our work had any relevance at all. For several months we continued, numbed by the experience of visiting the families, unable to think it through. (1988, 198)

Greg's impending "failure" in my composition course had nothing to do with writing ability, nothing to do with "just teaching writing," nothing much to do with the particular curriculum or pedagogy of my course, and everything to do with the politics of race and class, everything to do with the unequal distribution of even basic needs: food, shelter, health.

Glenda

Glenda started off well in my upper-division writing course. Although I don't grade individual papers, she was clearly in the top third of the class. She was particularly strong in her response groups, giving excellent and extensive responses to her fellow students.

As with the other two students, Glenda's troubles began with absences: two weeks straight, interrupted by one day in class where she was clearly subdued and troubled, and where she walked out quickly before I could talk to her. And then the office visit.

Glenda came in and said that she needed to explain why she was having difficulty coming to class. She was very clearly upset and nervous. She said that a man had raped her roommate and she had been staying home talking to her and trying to help her. She paused and then told me, "the same thing happened to me. I guess I haven't dealt with it. I thought I had, but this brings it back." She also told me that both she and her roommate knew who the man was, but they had not gone to the police. Then, absurdly, she said, "I tried to type your paper but my hands were shaking so bad. . . ."

We went to the judicial officer immediately and made an appointment at the counseling center. I remain haunted by the line about typing my paper. In the hierarchy of concerns in her life, I wonder why she was trying to type at all. As with Greg's story, I have hesitated to tell this story too. I don't seek out personal stories, and I'm not one of those teachers who thrives on personal relationships with students. Glenda's story isn't important because it's dramatic or sad. Nor is it irrelevant because it is rare. Men rape or attempt to rape nearly one in four women students on my campus. In addition to the terrible physical and psychological pain, rape is an *academic* problem, interfering with women's ability to achieve professional, intellectual, and political power through higher education.

The Responsibility of Composition Instruction

These narratives raise difficult questions about the responsibility of writing programs to increase access. They are not individual stories of individual problems. Rape doesn't happen to men, racism doesn't happen to whites, poverty doesn't happen to rich people. But these social and political problems have everything to do with providing access.

There are no easy answers here. Elspeth Stuckey's remarkable book, *The Violence of Literacy*, best illustrates both the problems and the difficulty of solutions. Stuckey passionately writes against the easy view that the acquisition of skills will provide access, claiming—counter to the intuition and desires of composition teachers—that the promise of literacy to provide access, because it is a false promise, is one of the ways that literacy does violence. Stuckey's argument, because it is counterintuitive, is difficult for many readers. While writing teachers have taken it on faith that literacy is liberatory, Stuckey argues just the opposite:

> Literacy, like communication, is a matter of access, a matter of opportunity, a matter of economic security—a total matter. The violence of literacy is the violence of the milieu it comes from, promises, recapitulates. It is attached inextricably to the world of food, shelter, and human equality. When literacy harbors violence, society harbors violence. To elucidate the violence of literacy is to understand the distance it forces between people and the possibilities for their lives. (1991, 94)

The stories of Greg, Alice, and Glenda document the inextricable attachment to material conditions that Stuckey refers to. They show how the violence of the everyday world enters into writing and literacy. It's a simple fact, but one that most writing teachers consider outside the realm of their responsibility.

In one sense, it is outside our responsibility. We can't expect writing instruction to save the world or even to intervene in the economic and social worlds that prevent Alice's, Greg's, and Glenda's full participation. That promise, since we can't keep it, is "violent." But there are some conclusions. First, if we are serious about increasing access to higher education for people of color in this country, then we first have to abandon the notion that skills alone provide access. Second, since social forces of inequality are so strong, we have to work with colleagues up and down the grade levels and across the curriculum to produce a citizenry that is committed to a new, more generous, more democratic society. Since social transformation on that scale through rhetorical methods is slow, discouraging, and nearly invisible, we must also be sure in the meantime, as Michael Holzman states, "to stop doing harm" whenever we can (1989, 138). This analysis should make it clear that, as writing teachers, we are institutionally positioned to gatekeep, to do harm. To create access, we must go against the grain.

Defining "stop doing harm" isn't easy in itself. This book takes that question in steps. First of all, through the political lens described by this chapter, I look at how issues of standards and access have been played out at important moments in the history of teaching writing.

Chapter Two

The Dialectic of Standards and Access in Nineteenth-Century Writing Instruction

In the second half of the nineteenth century in American universities and colleges, a unique course—composition—emerged from complex and broad political, economic, cultural, and institutional changes. These changes have shaped present conceptions of the complicated relationships between literacy, schooling, and social change. In perhaps the most fruitful burst of scholarship in composition's history, recent studies of nineteenth-century writing instruction have enabled new understandings of the complex and frequently contradictory demands of teaching writing in the present. The story of the birth of the first entrance exam at Harvard in 1876 and first-year composition in 1885 has been well-told by scholars such as Susan Miller, James Berlin, Wallace Douglas, Robert Connors, Richard Ohmann, and others. In this chapter, I will draw on their work to demonstrate how literacy instruction in institutional contexts was constrained by a series of ideologies governed by the basic concept of "remediation," and how remediation compromised access as a pedagogical, curricular, or political goal. Alongside this history, as a counterpoint, I have composed a history of the changing representations of literacy learning by African Americans, first under slavery and later during Reconstruction. Although these histories obtain their impact from different sources, their union in this chapter is one of conflict and contest, as well as coherence and connection. Ultimately, my wish is for these histories to illuminate the social and historical circumstances that gave birth to particular definitions of literacy as a means of access and standards as a means of exclusion.

The Composition Course at Harvard

The birth of composition is a classic case of overdetermination. The mid-nineteenth century marked a series of important changes in American society, not the least of which was the Civil War and resulting new pressures for a nation unified linguistically and culturally as well as geographically. This new national identity included an economic system that defined itself against the agrarian past and toward a modern, industrial future. This economic shift also entailed a reorganized social system that could accommodate changing class and cultural boundaries.

Composition histories written in the 1970s and early 80s, such as Douglas', Connors', Ohmann's, and even Berlin's, have tended to emphasize the economic pressures that influenced the curricular changes that resulted in first-year composition courses. In this economic explanation, current-traditional rhetoric was a vocational pedagogy, a part of the shift in higher education where "the professional aspects of a college education were beginning to rival the social aspects" (Connors 1986, 34). As industrialists began to accumulate vast amounts of wealth, they began to exert pressures on higher education to abandon its classical curriculum and create courses of study that would meet the needs of business and industry. "Men of affairs" replaced clergy and landed elite on university governing boards and, as Berlin notes, they argued for "an education that prepared students for work in this life, not for rewards in the next" (1984, 58–59). New industries also needed newly educated students; a broader band of students began to attend colleges and universities in response to the need for an educated managerial class. Berlin argues that the freshman composition course's inception and its attendant pedagogy, current-traditional rhetoric, was a response to these economic changes in American society and within American universities. Studies by Connors, Berlin, and others show how current-traditional pedagogy suited what industry thought they wanted, "a triumph of the scientific and technical world view" (Berlin 1984, 62). Writing instruction emphasized expository writing over other genres because that was the writing business and industry wanted (Berlin 1984, 63). It also encouraged "a mode of behavior that helps students in their move up the corporate ladder—correctness in usage, grammar, clothing, thought, and a certain sterile objectivity and disinterestedness" (Berlin 1984, 75).

This kind of writing instruction also fit a general cultural value of efficiency and scientific management in educational institutions. The emphasis on the "simply mechanical" fit a newly conceived split between "skill" and "conception." This rhetoric was also well-suited to enormously large classes (a working condition that Connors stresses) that early composition teachers faced, a material fact that had (and has)

contributed to paucity of theoretical depth. Current-traditional pedagogy initiated a limited conception of literacy education, one which reduced literacy to skills and reduced education to training.

But meeting the needs of the middle class and the new industrial
economy was only one of many pressures that universities faced. At the
beginning of the century what Gerald Graff calls "The Classical College"
was the dominant model (1987). University education was reserved for
the cultural elite and concentrated on the transmission of knowledge
necessary for the limited few who went to college as a part of the cus-
toms of their social class. This education was not particularly vocational,
but it was a part of the accretion of cultural markers that identified the
elite in a kind of cultural certification process. At Harvard, classical literacy instruction was for maintenance of leadership—moral, religious,
and intellectual. As Mary Trachsel argues, "College was a sort of finish-
ing school where [gentlemen's sons] prepared for the positions of aris-
tocratic leadership that came with inherited property and wealth . . .
and in an important sense this social value was also embodied in the
separate code of classical literacy" (1992, 32). The members of the colleges were already the elite, and literacy instruction simply helped
them fulfill their social roles. When the pressure from business and industry demanded that universities expand their traditional base of students and educate the middle class, this cultural certification could no
longer be central.

The pressure for increased access from business and industry dove-
tailed with structural changes in the ways that universities organized
themselves. In 1876, Johns Hopkins was founded as the first research
institution. In contrast to the other universities, Johns Hopkins organized its curriculum on specialized fields and courses of study—
what we now call majors—and emphasized graduate education over
undergraduate education. Other universities, Harvard—under Charles
William Eliot—Yale, and the University of Chicago soon followed this
model (Graff 1987, 56–57). Since graduate education and research are
much more expensive than undergraduate education, the economics of
this change also forced universities to make their curriculum attractive
to industrialists, and to fund their expensive graduate programs with
larger undergraduate enrollments. It resulted in increased specializa-
tions, especially in scientific and technical fields, and in an elective
system that by the end of the century at Harvard covered the entire
curriculum except first-year composition. The elective system that pre-
serves first-year composition as the sole nonelective produced a distinct relationship between composition courses and specialized courses.
Because of its particular institutional location as the sole nonelective
course *along with* the fundamentally remedial conception of its curricu-

lum, composition came to be seen as what now is called a "service" course—one whose privileged status as required ironically put it into bondage to other courses.

So from a number of directions, universities were pushed to provide increased access to middle-class students. It is easy to exaggerate the pressure for admitting the middle class to college, pressures from within the university and from business and industry. After all, as Connors shows, it was only a small percentage of the middle class that actually attended university (1991, 59). But it is important to imagine it from both the large view, where only a sliver of the populace attended college, and from within the university, where within the space of thirty years (1870 to 1900), the freshman class at Harvard tripled in size (Connors 1991, 69). To the formerly snug elite, this must have been the advancing hoards. They needed a buffer and so the exam system and later, freshman composition, were created as a moat to protect the castle within. The extent to which universities were committed (and still are) to this system is worthy of notice. Even at a time when college curricula were becoming elective-based, freshman composition remained, in many colleges and universities the one, single, requirement.

While access is usually a pragmatic adjustment to urgent economic or political pressures, the maintenance of standards is prompted by fear and defensiveness. This fear and defensiveness in the late nineteenth century was class- and culture-based, drawing on the newly defined sharpness of economic classes. Violent strikes by the working class and newspaper exposés of poverty and inhumane living conditions contrasted sharply with the opulent and ostentatious wealth of the industrialists. Institutional fear and defensiveness, not surprisingly, first took the form of an entrance examination, instituted at Harvard in 1874 and taken up by other colleges soon after.

So not only were the exam and the course connected with accommodating a newly industrialized economy and thus extending university education to the middle class, but also the exam and the course were caught in a conflict of values where industry money was valued, but middle-class students were not. David R. Russell—in one of the most succinct descriptions of this process—has called the accommodation of the two conflicting aims of composition courses, access and standards, a process of "institutionalizing ambiguity" (1992, 27). His description of this ambiguity bears repeating:

> General-composition courses have in one sense been a means of widening access by helping to "prepare" students for college work. But to the extent that those courses were treated as remedial or purgatorial, they also enforced a "gatekeeping" function by keeping students on the margins of the institution. (1992, 27)

In simple terms, the exam and the course, rather than providing a means of helping students to acquire the cultural markers of the university elite, served to exclude them altogether. Roughly one-half of the applicants failed Harvard's entrance exam. For those who passed, the course's curriculum, while perhaps suited to industry's needs, also served social and cultural purposes.

Reconceived as cultural work, the exam and course helped make distinctions between class and culture. More than fitting into industry's needs, the course—and current-traditional rhetoric—went about the social selection and certification of new students, the process that Miller calls "winnowing and indoctrination" (1991, 63). This view of freshman composition accounts for its placement at the beginning of the curriculum. That way if students failed to acculturate into academia, they could be told early on, and not contaminate the whole curriculum. The service nature of the course was not primarily academic; it was (and remains) social and cultural. This placement at the beginning of academic work ensconces composition as "purgatorial" or preliminary (Russell 1992, 27). Since it "serves" the other academic disciplines, its academic purposes remain unfocused and unwieldy. The first-year location, as Miller argues, tied the course to the entrance examination. And since the exam and the course were ushered into existence by a well-publicized complaint about the literacy abilities of students, the course was from the very beginning "on basically corrective, remedial ground" (1991, 63). Finally, the object of remediation was neither simply linguistic (all first-year students entering Harvard could both talk and write) nor academic (neither the exam nor the course purported to be about "subject matter," traditionally defined). Instead, its cultural work is well-summarized by Miller:

> [Composition was] a consciously selected menu to test students' knowledge of graphic conventions, to certify their propriety, and to socialize them into good academic manners. (1991, 66)

In her discussion of the pedagogy of these courses, Miller notes that the assignments moved from rhetorical modes of "comparison, contrast, classification, and the like" to more personal topics like "How I Learned to Like Good Music," a move that she characterizes as from "the sublime to the ridiculous" (1991, 59). And since these "ridiculous" topics were simply corrected, not substantively responded to, "both the written status of mechanically marked compositions and the content of those compositions were now reduced to objects of inconsequentiality" (1991, 59). This kind of curriculum, because it was not about knowledge in the traditional sense, focused mainly on style and a limited idea of style as manners, precisely a curriculum suited to screening for cultural markers used to sort students into "ready for Harvard" or not.

The exam and the curriculum in writing were also precisely the kind of nonacademic screen that would distinguish not only between working class and the elite, but screen students according to ethnic groups, too. The creation of freshman composition coincided with one of the great waves of immigration. The 1880s, especially, saw the immigration of Eastern Europeans to the United States for the first time. Although the classical curriculum was quickly disappearing from American colleges, the social use of higher education as a marker of cultural respectability was not so easily dispensed with. The newer, wealthy industrialist families saw higher education as a way to distinguish themselves from the class that they had recently exited. According to Lawrence Veysey,

> in these particular years of greatly expanding immigration from new and less respectable sources, "crude but vital" Anglo-Saxon families already established in America may well have felt a newly pronounced need to distinguish themselves by certain emphatic trademarks from those who stood below them on the social scale. A degree, particularly one which no longer required the bother of learning Greek or Latin, could become a tempting trademark of this sort—impressive, preeminently wholesome, and increasingly accessible to any family affluent enough to spare the earning power of its sons in their late teens. In these terms, an academic degree was like an insurance policy against downward mobility. (1965, 266)

Probably the most disturbing evidence for the cultural elitism in higher education in this era is the treatment of Jewish immigrants. The late 1880s and 1890s marked the beginning of the major immigration of Jews to the East Coast. Jews, especially from Western Europe, were fairly common in colleges and universities before this time. But this new group of Jewish immigrants were more culturally different. They came from more working-class environments. They tended to come from Eastern Europe instead of the more familiar, and more culturally privileged, Western Europe. They came tending to hold onto their traditions and not seek assimilation. Yet, as was true for many groups of immigrants during this period, they came with strong interests in education and, in particular, strong traditions in reading and writing. Despite stereotypical views that immigrants were the "dregs" of their societies of origin, Harvey Graff (and others) have shown that "Immigrants, students have come to recognize, were special kinds of people; literacy was among their distinctive characteristics" (1991, 65). Jews were no exception to this and they brought with them an additional cultural value of supporting institutionalized education for their families. Once these families achieved economic security in the United States, it was no surprise, then, that their children would attend higher education.

Given the tendency toward academic success, and given the social purposes of higher education to mark the elite and recently elite, and given that Eastern European Jews, especially, did not conform to the cultural norm, the colleges and universities were ripe for conflict. Stephen Steinberg shows how this conflict was set up:

> It was no doubt reflective of class formations elsewhere in society that higher education assumed features of a caste system. At the top of the hierarchy stood Harvard, Yale, Princeton, with Columbia struggling to retain its elite position. Within each institution was a wealthy class who dominated social life and set patterns imitated throughout the system of higher education. The leading institutions were measured more in terms of these status characteristics than by standards of scholarship and academic excellence.
>
> The important thing to be said about Jews is that they threatened this respectability. They did so, first of all, because they were lower-class, and frequently exhibited ethnic characteristics that violated what Veblen called, "the canons of genteel intercourse." Secondly, the seriousness and diligence with which they pursued their studies not only represented unwelcome competition, but implicitly called into question the propriety of a "gentlemen's college." Finally Jews were unwanted simply because they were Jews, and it was feared that their presence might diminish the social standing of the college and its students. (1974, 14–15)

The social standing of the college, in this case, seemed a fairly good predictor of antagonism toward Jews and other immigrants. The response by colleges and universities was at first subtle, but during the first part of the twentieth century, grew into direct quotas that limited the number of Jews who could attend.

What was at stake, and what the creation of freshman composition participated in, was the maintenance of the elite, not just of its members, but of its manners. That's why Miller's analysis of absence of content in the writing curriculum is so enlightening. If the purpose of the exam and course is to socialize, in the sense of inducting students into the academic community, and if the academic community's purpose has less to do with academics as we might now define it, then content would be irrelevant to the social agenda of the exam and course.

These social goals in the local administration of Harvard's composition program, and their work in "winnowing and indoctrinating" immigrants and working- and middle-class students, reflected larger social changes in attitudes toward language and literacy, specifically the development of the idea of "standard" language and what James Collins calls "universalistic" literacy. In the first part of the nineteenth century literacy standards were enforced locally, determined by efficacy in discrete situations. Good writing was good because it accomplished what it was supposed to do; it was measured by its efficacy in discrete situations. If a piece advised about methods for killing tobacco worms (Heath 1981, 27), and it did so, then it was a good piece of writing. Since most literate males had no education in literary texts, "good" in the aesthetic sense was a foreign concept. Instead, "good" was a utilitarian concept, well suited to the Ben Franklin-like values of the age. "Good" was also divorced from an individual. The sense of a style residing in a individual's skills was not important, for individual pieces were frequently not even signed, or signed with a generic pseudonym such as "an American" (Heath 1981, 28–29).

This sense of writing and writing standards changed in the later nineteenth century. According to Collins (1989) and Heath (1981), standards became associated with nationalism, patriotism, and common schools, and thus became prescriptive and unitary. According to Collins,

> This latter generalized prescriptivism, in which the standard came to be viewed as a symbol of nationalist authenticity, occurs during the period of national consolidation in the post-Civil War United States, a time when stringent monolingualism also became the official language policy of the emerging empire. (1989, 14)

Collins' work is especially valuable to this study because he focuses not only on the consequences of the development of a "standard," but the complex processes by which the standard continues to be legitimated. He states that there are three complementary processes that joined to create the current idea of "standard" and its reproduction: "the association of language with national unification; the association of literacy with mobility; and the indexical fixing of an authoritative literate tradition" (27).

These three processes of legitimation broaden the analysis of the context that created freshman composition and complement the analyses of Miller, Berlin, and other historians of composition. Collins claims that standard language emerged as a part of the process of nationalization in the second half of the nineteenth century. To underscore the strength of the social and political forces working to establish a national identity, one only needs to remember that a war was fought over the idea. Certainly, the Civil War, more than any other event during this time, required the nation to assess, create, and enforce ideas of common identity, for the "United States," as a concept, now not only had to include "conquered" Southern states, but newly enfranchised slaves, whose status as citizens was contested both in the North and the South. With a new reorganization of nationhood, including more broadly distributed public schooling, decentralized, utilitarian standards for written language changed to reflect a single standard of what Collins calls "schooled literacy." Standards, in Collins' phrase, became "text-indexed"—the second process of standardization—instead of embedded in situations, purposes, and effects. This standard became more aesthetic, more based on literary models than on everyday use. Since a national literature is one of the means of creating a national identity, we should not find it surprising that the organized study of vernacular literature also originated during this time (Graff 1987), and as Susan Miller points out, originated as the opposing "other" to composition, the "high" to composition's "low" (1991, 51–55). This emerging nationalism and the standards accompanying it engendered what Robert Connors in "The Rhetoric of Mechanical Correctness" calls "the first great period of linguistic insecurity" (1986, 30). Language, for the first time in this country, began to help accomplish the task of making and maintaining class distinctions. Standardization worked as Raymond Williams argues it does in *Keywords:* "to convict a majority of native speakers of English of speaking their own language 'incorrectly'" (1983, 297).

Shirley Brice Heath's "Towards an Ethnohistory of Writing in American Education" makes essentially the same claims as Collins. Writing in the early nineteenth century flourished, and, according to Heath, included working-class people: "During the colonial and early national periods, working-class people produced highly literate political documents and responses to political, social, and economic proposals of the local and national government" (1981, 27). Heath documents widespread public literacy practices that include political commentary, how-to documents, and letter writing. By the end of the century, however, only letter writing, the most private of the kinds of writing she documents, remained a widespread practice. Heath attributes this change to the appropriation of writing instruction from the community to the schools. As writing ceased to be measured by utility and began to be measured more abstractly, against literary models, public writing by ordinary citizens declined. Additionally, and supportive of Miller's claims that writing became a site for sorting and indoctrination, Heath shows how writing—and excellence in writing—became attached to the values of the author, "good men wrote good compositions" (34). The result was that standards of text evaluation worked to discriminate class and culture: "those who wrote and criticized well had more intelligence, morality, and industry than did their fellow students. A class consciousness was developing on the basis of language used and the standards of writing perpetuated in the classroom" (35). This discriminating practice relied almost entirely upon formal features of language. According to Heath, "Composition students were asked to write on topics about which they had little or no real information: aspects of morality or immorality, idleness, the talent of success, or order in school" (35). The focus on style, as Miller has pointed out, worked to devalue the pragmatic and political functions of writing as knowledge making or communicating and to heighten writing's aesthetic value, making writing much more suited to the business of class and cultural discrimination.

Literacy, Standardization, and Access

It may seem contradictory that a rhetoric of mobility or access should accompany the creation of freshman composition and the development of a standardized language. Collins describes the development of the "standard" as a hegemonic process, not directly oppressive. In other words, new literacy standards and the freshman composition course that accompanied their development needed a rhetoric that would make these oppressive developments seem palatable, maybe even advantageous, to the working and middle classes. The rhetoric used is the rhetoric of access. The argument was that class differences (and, in other contexts, race differences) can be overcome through the mastery of ruling-class language. In other words, all one had to do to be a "son of Harvard" was to talk and write like one. Accordingly, the process of talking and writing like a son of Harvard was purely a mechanical, neutral process. Collins states that as literacy became more and more "nationalized," it also became more "linked to ideals of social mobility" (1989, 14). The argument, as old as freshman composition and as young as yesterday, is that anyone can master a neutral language and that this mastery will create "equal opportunity." This is Graff's "Literacy Myth" or Stuckey's "Violence of Literacy." There is not much evidence—statistical or anecdotal—to support the view that language alone creates opportunity and a great deal of evidence against it, as argued in Chapter 1. Language is socially located and works to demarcate social boundaries. Economic and social power *precede* school success, not the other way around. But the rhetoric of social mobility, the rhetoric of access, worked in conjunction with the emergence of national standards. Bruce Herzberg, in "Composition and the Politics of the Curriculum," argues that arguments for "equal opportunity" helped to defuse class conflicts by depoliticizing the curriculum. As long as there were those exceptions who seemed by virtue of their schooling to transcend their class origins, the cultural work of schooling and especially literacy pedagogy was obscured and free from criticism. Herzberg writes that this sense of the relationship between national literacy standards (which were touted as neutral and whose class origins were suppressed) and social mobility was embodied in the "current-traditional," technical composition course:

> In the technically-oriented curriculum, knowledge is treated as a neutral set of skills and facts, accessible, presumably, to anyone. Failure means the student's failure to apply himself to the task. Failure is therefore the student's responsibility. For college students at the turn of the century and the first decades of the twentieth century, this form of applied Calvinism was a test of the individual's pretensions to learning, and perhaps not an unreasonable test. After all, college promised a

certain kind of success, and a certain kind of knowledge and skill was its price. Even so, this approach to teaching—especially in the public schools and in colleges later in the century—legitimates the traditional culture of the privileged classes by treating it as a neutral fact. (1991, 109–110)

This is a troubled history, to say the least. Composition as a discipline has identified itself almost entirely with the freshman course, and it has labored under the ideology of the course as a gate, a test, a service to industry, a site of a rather peculiar socialization focused on "manners."

Although many other developments in the teaching of composition occurred during and after the nineteenth century, the structure of the course as a required entry-level screen and socializer remains. Placement tests supporting these goals have, if anything, proliferated (and show no signs of abating). Although portfolio examinations are obviously more relevant than either grammar exams or timed writing tests, portfolio exams still are "winnowing" devices set only for writing. Despite the fact that required courses have made a comeback in many disciplinary areas, writing remains the only area where additional safeguards against those "in need of scrubbing" (Miller 1991, 85) remain in place. These features of our current academic landscape testify to the enduring construction of writing as a means of deciding the worthy from the unworthy. Those courses for students who "fail" the placement tests are—structurally, if not pedagogically—courses in coercive socialization.

An Undiscoursed History of Writing

While Donald Stewart's argument in "Harvard's Influence on English Studies" convinces me that Harvard's writing course is the single most influential history to be told, other arguments about the "highly differentiated" (Schulz 1994, 10) landscape of history show us that while Harvard's course and the pedagogy that emerged from it were powerful, there are always other histories to be told. For instance, Donald Stewart, James Berlin, and others have showed the remarkable career of F. N. Scott who resisted nearly every move that Harvard made and whose theories anticipated aspects of the expressivists and the social constructivists.

Additionally, composition has begun to turn its attention to the histories of writing outside of the established curriculum. For instance, Anne Ruggles Gere's 1993 Conference on College Composition and Communication (CCCC) presidential address, "Kitchen Tables and Rented Rooms: The Extracurriculum of Composition," called attention to the growing trend to imagine the history of composition as larger than the kinds of institutional histories that have informed the first part of this chapter. She argues that by concentrating on institutional contexts for constructing composition's history, we have neglected other powerful contexts for learning to write. And although the term "extracurriculum" first referred to the clubs and societies that attached themselves to academic institutions, Gere extends the definition (and thus the social groups under study):

> . . . my version of the extracurriculum includes the present as well as the past; it extends beyond the academy to encompass the multiple contexts in which persons seek to improve their own writing; it includes more diversity in gender, race, and class among writers. . . . (1994, 80)

The project of writing a less institutionally focused history of composition may serve institutional instruction by extending our consciousness of writing instruction beyond the oppressive model provided by Harvard. For students and teachers in composition classes in today's universities and colleges, the expansive histories of the extracurriculum in composition could provide promising models of teaching and learning, models that could attract and retain a broader range of our social strata, models that could shift the historically fundamental definition of composition as remedial in purpose and in service to other academic disciplines.

Composition originated in the repudiation of writing in everyday, public uses, i.e., writing in the broadly defined extracurriculum. By writing about the literacy practices of African Americans in nineteenth-century America, I'm hoping to claim this history as a generative force as we construct pedagogies, curricula, and writing programs in the late twentieth century. Susan Miller makes the point in *Textual Carnivals* that "actual writing" is "undiscoursed" (1991, 34); that is nonacademic writing is excluded from formal histories of writing and rhetoric. With few exceptions, the history of composition is only the history of institutionalized instruction. This historiographical exclusion functions politically to legitimate reductive views of writing and writing instruction, the particular social and political agenda that helped form these views (see Miller 1991, 34–35).

Claiming literacy practices of African Americans as a part of composition instruction's history, produces a rupture in the institutionalized history of composition. Because of the specificity of the historical conditions of African American literacy, this history can generate a "composition" that defines learning to write in terms of specific political goals that see writing as a struggle for freedom rather than a means of social exclusion.

Writing, Freedom, and Repression

An obvious feature of African American literacy in the pre–Civil War South was that it was more transparently political than literacy for whites. Despite threats of dismemberment (cutting off the index finger was a common punishment for slaves who were caught writing), whipping, and even death, African Americans learned to read and write in remarkable numbers. From 5 to 10 percent of slaves could read and write. Based on her extensive examination of a variety of sources, Janet Duitsman Cornelius, in her important book, *When I Can Read My Title Clear,* has argued that the 10 percent figure is more likely the accurate one.

That any significant population of slaves learned to read and write testifies to the strength and ingenuity of slave resistance, considering the violent opposition to slave literacy. In the 1830s, following various publicized slave rebellions, fearful white Southerners believed that literacy contributed centrally to rebellion and enacted legislation that made teaching and learning literacy illegal. South Carolina, which historically had banned slave literacy in 1740 and in 1800, had one of the most restrictive of laws. The discussion that preceded its enactment in 1834 continually referred to the role that literacy played in the elaborately organized scheme for rebellion in Charleston eight years before planned by the literate slave, Denmark Veysey. Slave-owner Whitemarsh Seabrook, whom Cornelius calls "fussy and somewhat pedantic," unrelentingly led the movement to ban literacy teaching to slaves. His tactics were to argue that literacy and religion were the two main threats to slave-owners' power and were "most dangerous when combined" (1991, 40). During the years 1829 through 1834, Georgia, Louisiana, North Carolina, Virginia, Alabama, and South Carolina all passed these laws. Most laws included prohibitions to assemble as well.

While the legal suppression of literacy learning was difficult to enforce, antiliteracy laws were a symbolic gesture that signified the collective fear that slave-owners had about reading and writing, and legitimated (for them) the violent means used to punish slaves for learning to read and write. These laws were in part aimed at Northern abolitionists who wished to teach slaves to read and write. Brutal slave-owners, however, never needed laws to enforce their wishes. Cornelius cites several stories of slaves who told of the punishments—from whipping, to amputating fingers to prevent writing, to hanging—for getting caught reading and writing (66). It was clear to any slave in the early nineteenth century that reading and writing were risks.

Apparently, slave-owners had a reason to fear literacy. They cited the fact that rebellious leadership among slaves, from Nat Turner to Denmark Vesey in Charleston, saw printed texts—abolitionist texts, biblical texts, newspaper reports of slave rebellions—as "an inspiration for revolt" (Cornelius 1991, 30). They cited David Walker's *Appeal in Four Articles*, a passionate and powerful exhortation to revolt, as further evidence.

Walker's text was especially troublesome to them. According to the "Brief Sketch of the Life and Character of David Walker" that accompanies the 1848 edition, the *Appeal* "caused more commotion among slaveholders than any volume of its size that was ever issued from an American press" (Walker [1848] 1969, vi). It's not hard to see why. Walker's *Appeal* strikes at the heart of all slaveholder's fears. First of all, it is addressed to "Colored Citizens" and assumed a literate slave audience. This rhetorical move excludes white readers, placing the issues of freedom and liberty out of their control. Walker repeatedly addresses his audience as "my beloved brethren," and sometimes even more pointedly selects his audience: "Men of colour, who are also of sense, for you particularly is my appeal designed" (Walker [1848] 1969, 40). For the planters to imagine an audience in the way that Walker demands they imagine it, would be to destroy their image of slaves as subhuman. By way of brilliantly critiquing, not the most racist planters, but "moderate" arguments such as Jefferson's section on slavery in *Notes on the State of Virginia* and Henry Clay's plan for Liberian colonization, Walker repeatedly argues for open insurrection. His image of literacy is, I believe, representative:

> You have to prove to the Americans and the world, that we are MEN, and not *brutes* as we have been represented, and by millions treated. Remember, to let the aim of your labours among your brethren, and particularly the youths, be the dissemination of education and religion. . . . Some few of them, may make out to scribble tolerably well, over half a sheet of paper, which I believe has hitherto been a powerful obstacle in our way, to keep us from acquiring knowledge. ([1848] 1969, 42)

This "knowledge," Walker makes clear, is knowledge of the brutality of slavery, knowledge that will "make the tyrants quake and tremble" (44). Literacy has power because slave-owners will know that "their infernal deeds of cruelty will be made known to the world" (44). Additionally, Walker argues that once educated, slaves will no longer tolerate slave conditions:

> Do you suppose one man of good sense and learning would submit himself, his father, mother, wife and children, to be slaves to a wretched man like himself, who, instead of compensating him for his labours, chains, handcuffs and beats him and family almost to death, leaving life enough in them, however, to work for, and call him master? No! no! . . . The bare name of educating the coloured people, scares our cruel oppressors almost to death. ([1848] 1969, 44)

Walker's rhetorical identification with slaves, his knowledge of history, his skills in argumentation, his unrelenting assertions of African American humanity and power, and the widespread dissemination of his pamphlet, gave Southern planters good reason to fear literacy.

The slave-owning South, both the legislative and social power structure, seemed to understand this role that literacy could play in challenging oppression. While it is difficult to imagine in the 1990s, given the reductionist views of literacy today, literacy was at the very center of the debate about slavery in the 1830s. African American slaves and freedmen sought literacy as a means of challenging and transforming their communities and the nation. In doing so, they shook the ideological underpinnings of Southern slavery.

In the face of a threatened and determined opposition, slaves felt very powerful motives for writing. Many, if not most, of these motives were pragmatically political, but I'll begin with one that may seem less immediately so. One of the means of political action was resisting the definitions of (in)humanity imposed on slaves by white society. As many commentators on literacy have pointed out, literacy in the Western world has been associated with the very quality of being a human. The racist beliefs that allowed slavery to exist defined slaves as subhuman, incapable of or unsuited to many intellectual tasks, not the least of which was literacy, and especially writing. Robert Stepto, in *From Behind the Veil*, argues that the reason that many slave narratives had to be "authenticated" by white people was that their audience, while perfectly willing to believe that slaves could be free, had difficulty believing that slaves could write. Charles T. Davis and Henry Louis Gates, Jr. concur, arguing that the slave narrative "arose as a response to and a refutation of claims that slaves *could* not write" (1985, xv). The act of writing itself, for a slave, challenged the ideological structure of slavery.

Writing also involved an assertion of a collective identity that the removal from Africa, the separation of families, and the various laws that prevented assembly (many of which accompanied antiliteracy laws), made urgent. Opposition to the very humanity of slaves, paradoxically, made writing more urgently important. Davis and Gates write:

> The slave narrative represents the attempts of blacks to *write themselves into being*. What a curious idea: through the mastery of formal Western languages, the presupposition went, a black person could become a human being by an act of self-creation through the mastery of language. Accused of having no collective history by Hegel in 1813, blacks responded by publishing hundreds of individual histories. (1985, *xxiii*)

Literacy—especially writing—carried with it this oppositional stance. For instance, Frederick Douglass' master opposed his learning to read and write, which made Douglass all the more determined to become literate. He credits his accomplishment to the opposition of his master: "In learning to read, therefore, I am not sure that I owe as much to the opposition of my master as to the kindly assistance of my mistress" (quoted in Cornelius 1991, 1). Thomas Webber, in *Deep Like the Rivers,* claims that "the efforts of the white community to discourage the learning attempts of their slaves only strengthened the slaves' resolve" (1978, 135). He cites the experience of Austin Steward as representative; after he was flogged for studying a book, Steward reported:

> [I]nstead of giving me the least idea of giving it up, only made me look upon it as a more valuable attainment. Else, why should my oppressor feel so unwilling that their slaves should possess that which they thought so essential to themselves? (quoted in Webber 1978, 135)

Literacy was an individual and collective argument against the various, increasingly absurd defenses of slavery in the early nineteenth century. The assertion of collection identity was not as much a psychological act as it was a political act against slavery.

Most of the reasons that African Americans claimed for learning to read and write were pragmatic. Writing, in particular, was linked with freedom in the form of a pass. So entrenched in the belief that slaves could not write, a slave could write himself a "pass" that would allow him mobility or facilitate his escape. Although Frederick Douglass' autobiography is the most famous example of a slave writing his own pass, many other slave narratives tell similar tales. Passes could be used to gain time to escape to the North, or, as Cornelius notes, could be used to gain temporary freedom to visit family members in other locations.

Writing became identified with freedom on this individual level, but it also became a part of the collective struggle, as the pamphlets of Walker and others show. African Americans wrote—and read—to be involved with the ongoing struggle for collective freedom. This first protest literature took many forms: political pamphlets, slave narratives, court petitions for emancipation, and written accounts of slave rebellions. The volume and force of this literature tied literacy—in both the slave populations and in white slave-owners—with resistance.

This brief account of literacy learning among African Americans in slavery seems, and is, a dramatic contrast to the institutional history of composition. Chronologically, the pre–Civil War period predates most common public schools, predates the sense of nationalism that was a consequence of the Civil War, and predates the linguistic standardization of the second half of the century. The context of African Americans' literacy, the fact that it worked against and outside dominant institutions, gave it a particular stamp of urgency, and of action, and perhaps, political effectiveness, too.

Emancipation and the Domestication of Literacy

Some white Southerners saw the unbridled nature of African American literacy as its most dangerous feature. Instead of arguing for antiliteracy laws, which they perceived would be ineffective (correctly, since literacy learning had gone on outside the purview of repressive masters), many white Southerners argued that the best way to preserve slavery would be to institutionalize literacy. For instance, in the public discussions preceding South Carolina's antiliteracy laws, some Southern whites argued that formal schooling for slaves would better control the content of their learning and make slaves more submissive, industrious, and accepting (Cornelius 1991, 45–46).

Regardless of Southern whites' wishes, institutionalized schooling and literacy instruction came soon enough. As soon as Northern armies began to conquer Southern lands, slaves were set free. And as soon as slaves were set free, a wide variety of people with vastly different sets of purposes began to set up schools. Ultimately, these schools were governed by a federal agency, the Freedmen's Bureau. The Freedmen's Bureau was originally created to deal with the immediate needs of freed slaves, such as food, shelter, and health. Within a year of its creation, the Freedmen's Bureau concentrated on education to the exclusion of other more urgent political issues (such as land and franchise). This sole concentration on education as the one means to equality deserves scrutiny. Most scholars of education—with the notable exception of Ronald Butchart's *Northern Schools, Southern Blacks, and Reconstruction*—see the Freedmen's Bureau's activities as anomalous in the otherwise persistent neglect or antagonism towards African American education in our history as a whole. They note that the freedmen's schools brought over 2,500 teachers (many of them Northern white women) to the South to teach newly enfranchised slaves (Butchart 1980, 4). And as the first system of institutionalized instruction in literacy to African Americans in this country, the freedmen's schools altered the symbolic—and actual—role that literacy had played in the lives of African Americans.

In the pre–Civil War time, literacy for African Americans symbolized freedom by contradicting the dominant class' definition of Africans as subhuman. Once emancipated, freedmen retained these ideas about literacy. They attended freedmen's schools in droves and at great sacrifice. Teachers were faced with class sizes from fifty to one hundred, and many children and adults were turned away. Teacher after teacher remarked on the seriousness of their students. Butchart writes: "The intense desire for knowledge and literacy was reflected in the classroom. Teachers and observers marveled at the freedmen's zealous application to schoolwork, rapid advancement, and evidence of mental equality with whites" (1980, 170). Northern teachers, steeped in the same racist ideologies as the South, were particularly astonished to find ex-slaves already reading and writing. James Anderson sees this fact as evidence of the "former slaves' fundamental belief in the value of literate culture" and their determination "to secure schooling for themselves and their children" (1988, 5).

The motives for attending freedmen's schools were much the same as motives for learning literacy before emancipation. Freedmen went to school to achieve practical power. It was as much a part of the collective movement for freedom as before slavery. Ex-slaves learned to read and write so that they could read their employment contracts and, for the lucky, the papers that allowed them to own property, so that they could participate in a newly opened political process, and so that they could foster collective race pride. Ex-slaves also retained the ideological, and symbolic understanding of literacy from the days of enslavement. In the words of James Anderson, "emancipation extruded an ex-slave class with a fundamentally different consciousness of literacy [from whites], a class that viewed reading and writing as a contradiction of oppression" (1988, 17).

Ultimately, both the practical political ends of education and the ideological hope for equality through education were betrayed in the years after the Civil War. Both the planters in the South, and the Northern reformers had significantly different ideas for schools in the South from the ex-slaves. Schools were central to the Freedmen's Bureau, in fact, after a year of its existence, schools were just about all that the Freedmen's Bureau was engaged in. Reconstruction had promised land reform and a fundamental redistribution of wealth. It had promised real opportunity. In the years shortly after the war, one by one, the bureau and the nation—and the Southern planters who regained their dominance—turned their backs on real reforms, leaving only schooling. Butchart is most succinct on this point:

> The Afro-Americans were on the threshold of freedom. They needed land, protection, and a stake in society. They needed and demanded meaningful power. They were given instead a school. The gift was vastly inadequate to the needs of men and women set free in a vengeful, vindictive society. Indeed, as the school fell under the control of a race and a class with interests opposed to those of southern blacks, education was not merely inadequate, it was utterly inappropriate. (1980, 9)

As the Freedmen's Bureau became more and more concerned with schools, and as it took control of even the schools run by blacks, literacy instruction for ex-slaves switched from literacy for liberation to literacy for social control. Curricular materials from the freedmen's schools clearly show the stress on manners and individual industry. While capitalizing on motives for demonstrating "humanity" and achieving economic freedom, the texts for freedmen represent literacy in a fundamentally different and conflicting light from the image of literacy as liberating. Some of the schools used the same textbooks as white schools, while others used materials specifically created for freedmen's schools. These materials, as would be expected, vary according to the ideological leanings of the groups who published and used them. Since many of the freedmen's schools were founded by evangelical aid societies, the readers reflected religious values of temperance, piety, and domesticity. In most cases, very few texts addressed the conditions of slaves or the conditions of freedom. The more conservative books, those published by the American Tract Society (ATS), did address slavery and freedom, but avoided all criticism of planters and presented the freedmen in demeaning ways: lazy, unkempt, docile, dependent, mentally inferior, always in the role of an agricultural laborer. Prior to the war, the ATS published numerous religious tracts, but in no way could the organization be considered antislavery. Its materials reflected its opposition to black equality.

The ATS readers stand out in contrast to another choice for freedmen, Lydia Maria Child's *The Freedmen's Book*. In many ways, Child's book extends the ideology of literacy that the slaves held prior to the war. Child's story, "The Meeting in the Swamp," for instance, draws upon the ways that collectivity and literacy served liberation. It is the story of a slave-owner, Mr. Duncan, who follows a slave to a secret meeting. There he witnesses a man who proclaims that "at last I finds out how de white man always git he foot on de black man" ([1865]1968, 108). The man's answer is literacy and he holds up the newspaper to show it. He describes learning to read by tricking his master's son; he describes the use of reading in order to inform himself and his fellow slaves about possible political developments that pertain to their freedom.

More than other readers, Child's selections (most written by herself) openly criticize slaveholders. In "The Beginning and Progress of Emancipation in the British West Indies," Child takes particular aim at West Indian slave-owners who kept their slaves "in brutal ignorance." She ridicules the response of the slave-owners to missionaries intent on teaching Bible literacy: "They said if slaves were instructed they would rise in rebellion against their masters. The English people replied that it must be a very bad system which made it dangerous for human beings to read the Bible" ([1865]1968, 128). Additionally, in her biographies of Madison Washington and Frederick Douglass, Child represents literacy learning as, in part, an act of rebellion.

Certainly, by the very inclusions of writing by Francis W. Harper, Frederick Douglass, Phyllis Wheatly, and other African Americans, and the more open representation of the cruelty of slave-owners and the resistance of slaves through literacy, Child's text differs from both Mc-Guffey's readers, which were used throughout the freedmen's schools, and the more conservative texts from ATS. Yet *The Freedmen's Book* also represents literacy learning as more domesticating than liberating. In the final essay, "Advice From an Old Friend," Child stresses the power of individual character as a means of political reform. She claims that her biographies of black revolutionaries "prove that the power of *character* can overcome all external disadvantages, even that most crushing of disadvantages, Slavery" (emphasis in the original [[1865]1968, 269]). The content of this character prevents the kinds of critical incisiveness or collective action that would have served the freedmen's political needs at the time. Child's essay argues for the following (not surprising) features of character, and makes her claims for the validity of these features on the biographies of black revolutionaries that she herself wrote. She argues that for emancipation to be successful, the ex-slaves needed to be "sober, industrious, and honest." She devotes paragraphs to the virtues of manners, personal appearance, and thriftiness. And while these characteristics veer significantly from the pragmatic education of the slaves, they are couched in similar political frames. After informing her readers that slavery remains legal in other countries, Child relates the following lesson on the virtues of tidy homes:

> . . . if your homes look neat, and your clothes are clean and whole, and your gardens well weeded, and your work faithfully done, whether for yourselves or others, then all the world will cry out, "You see that negroes *can* take care of themselves; and it is a sin and a shame to keep such men in Slavery." ([1865]1968, 270)

In addition to being insufficient political advice, the use of this story in a pedagogical context sets up a sharply divided sense of literacy, one originating in slavery that builds on a real and symbolic connection with liberation, yet one that also misuses that connection by displacing the tremendous political needs of the ex-slaves for political power into the domain of individual manners.

Of course, a curriculum is not the same thing as an education. There is no evidence that the ex-slaves took Child's advice and traded in political action for planter boxes in front of their homes. Indeed, most of the evidence suggests a great deal of resistance to white teachers in general. Anderson's history of black education is the most thorough on this point. Even before the establishment of the Freedmen's Bureau, ex-slaves had set up schools for themselves. Thomas Alvord, superintendent of schools for the Freedmen's Bureau, found a whole system of black-initiated, black-run schools. Du Bois, Woodson, and others all point to this system as the foundation of public education in the South. The freedmen showed a clear preference for black teachers, too, sometimes offending Northern teachers. This preference stemmed from deep mistrust of whites, to be sure, but also from a desire to resist "external control," and, according to Anderson, test "their capacity to restructure their lives, to establish their freedom" (1988, 12).

For Northerners as well as for Southerners, the Civil War and the potential political and social enfranchisement of the freedmen broke open their world. Reconstruction promised a radically new political and social system. Literacy for African Americans was a part of this new society, though by no means as important for political transformation as land ownership or voting rights. Yet the remarkable, perhaps unprecedented, commitment to schooling reflected a continued belief in the power of literacy to "help raise the freed people to an appreciation of their historic responsibility to build a better society and that any significant reorganization of the southern political economy was indissolubly linked to their education in the principles, duties, and obligations appropriate to a democratic social order" (Anderson 1988, 28).

One can hardly imagine a greater contrast than the ways that literacy was constructed at Harvard during this time period and the ways that literacy was constructed in the slave communities. Outside of schools and outside of any dominant institution—outside the hope of "access" to these institutions—slave literacy was less concerned with demonstrating "manners" associated with class or privilege and more concerned with political action.

These two histories, the development of the composition course at Harvard, and the changing symbolic representation of literacy for African Americans in the nineteenth century, had little contact with each other. African Americans did not attend Harvard, nor did they attend universities that were significantly affected by Harvard's course in writing. There are some parallels. The extracurricular history of writing for both blacks and whites in the early nineteenth century (as documented by Heath, Collins, and Cornelius) reveals a conception of literacy as a political and social practice, and standards of literacy that were local and related to the success of the political practice. "Good" writing, initially, was simply writing that got the job done. To slaves reading David Walker's appeals, it was good writing because it incited collective action. Neither white nor black literacy was learned primarily in the schools. For a variety of reasons—nationalism, the common school movement, fear of immigrants and blacks, and the working class, the rise of vernacular literature as a standard of literacy, and so on—literacy after the Civil War for both blacks and whites became a matter of character and manners. Heath's remark that "good men wrote good compositions" was equally true of the standards of literacy promoted by the freedmen's texts. Obvious political and pragmatic concerns dropped off in the second part of the century, replaced by more abstract standards based on Northern ruling-class ideas of character and morality. Literacy rooted in collective or community action was replaced by a litany of individual manners and morality. Content became less important; style, in perhaps the most limited sense imaginable, ascended. In short, once literacy was institutionalized it became more clearly a tool for ideological oppression.

In some senses the argument I am making seems ridiculously, even offensively, obvious. No clandestine meetings of slaves—risking torture, dismemberment, or death—would "practice" literacy by composing essays on "The First Snowstorm of the Year" (Miller 1991, 59). Instead, teaching and learning were tied directly to a real purpose: copying passes, as Henry Bibb did, for instance. But once institutional writing instruction was made available to ex-slaves and made available with rhetoric that drew upon established notions about the connections between freedom and literacy, then these "obvious" notions about writing instruction grew into a betrayal of the rhetoric of emancipation through the curriculum and pedagogy of selection, indoctrination, and gatekeeping. "Emancipation" changed from an actual process of writing to a once-removed process of admission and acculturation. The standards of admission and acculturation were (and in many respects *remain*) a driving force that more often reproduce the academic manners of the elite.

These two histories occurred in separate parts of the country, nearly in two separate countries, and in two classes of people who had little meaningful contact with each other. The histories never really met until desegregation in the late 1950s in public education and not until the early 1970s in higher education when the Open Admissions movement let African Americans and other students of color into the university in large numbers for the first time.

Chapter Three

Ideologies of Access and Exclusion

Basic Writing and Cultural Conflict

Composition's institutional origins in the late-nineteenth century are—like it or not—the framework within which issues of access and gate-keeping standards occur. The balance of these two concerns has tipped one way and then the other across the decades, depending on the needs of industry and democratic pressures from students, soldiers, and progressives. Although a case could be made for the radical transformation of higher education that accompanied the G.I. Bill in the 1950s, the most serious challenge to the rhetoric of gatekeeping was made in the early 1970s when "equal access" ascended to the level of official policy in the Open Admissions movement. It began when City University of New York decided in mid-1969 to change dramatically their admissions policy. The new policy, Open Admissions, rejected standardized test scores and grades as admission standards. Such a change radically challenged all the colleges of the system, but nowhere was that challenge felt more keenly than at City College. It was a radical and hopeful educational experiment, despite its failings—a historical sign that large scale change is possible. It paired a critique of standardized measures of performance with a possibility that the university could work against social inequality. As a key part of this historical scene was the remarkable (to 1990s eyes) sense of power that students of color felt and exercised. All involved with Open Admissions—critics and advocates—agreed that African American students especially but also Latino students led the way for Open Admissions and were almost entirely responsible for its early implementation.

I trace many of the most salutary developments in composition studies to Open Admissions: the exploration of home and school discontinuities, the interpretive study of student writing, the rejection of standardized tests as an accurate measure of writing ability, and the study of discourse communities in educational contexts. Additionally, Open Admissions posed a strong challenge to the existing role of higher education as socially reproductive. And it was temporarily successful in attracting students of color, and especially African Americans into higher education. The percentage of African Americans attending CUNY rose from 12.3 just before Open Admissions to nearly 35 percent in just a few years. This rosy view of Open Admissions is mitigated by the abandonment of the experiment only a few years after it began, in large measure forced out because of budget cuts.

Open Admissions was boldly and openly a political action—a more than ordinary resolve to intervene in the history of higher education that I explored in the last chapter. It seemed to tip the scale away from gatekeeping and toward access. One of its primary goals was inviting students of color into the university. Guideline 4 established by the Board of Higher Education of the City College of New York states that Open Admissions "shall result in the ethnic integration of the colleges" (Rossman et al. 1975, 9). Such a certain commitment to "ethnic integration" strikes me as freshly optimistic, courageously aware of the role that higher education *could* play in the lives of people of color in this country. Such a goal, though it may strike us as wildly optimistic, nonetheless imagined the university in a social, historical, and political context; it recognized historical racism and its effects and sought to intervene in the historical scene.

This guideline is preceded in the list by Guideline 3, which states that Open Admissions "shall maintain and enhance the standards of academic excellence of the colleges of the university" (Rossman et al. 1975, 9). The coexistence of these two items on this list together demonstrates again that standards and access are ideologically paired.

This is the "institutionalized ambiguity" that Russell described in reference to general composition at Harvard, the conflict between gatekeeping and access. Shaughnessy, in the opening sentence of *Errors and Expectations*, outlines the view of Open Admissions from precisely this vantage point: "Toward the end of the sixties and largely in response to protests of that decade, many four-year colleges began admitting students who were not by traditional standards ready for college" (1977, 1).

Standards almost always reflect an extension of the past into the future, because standards invariably reflect the values of those in power during times of change. There is no need to assert standards when they are comfortably in place, and talk about standards usually reflects a conservative fear that changes are taking place. So while Guideline 4 asserts a change, Guideline 3 attempts to forestall that change. Given the institutional fear of the middle class that drove the creation of freshman composition at Harvard, it isn't difficult to draw a parallel here. To almost entirely white professors, the thousands of students of color poised to enter City College did indeed threaten the status quo. Both 1885, when Harvard instituted its Freshman composition course, and 1970, when CUNY initiated Open Admissions, were historical moments when forces for change clashed dramatically with institutions that resisted change. These moments of political tensions are signaled by linguistic issues (just as when slavery was threatened, literacy laws dominated the political discourse), and in university and school contexts these tensions become focused on writing instruction. In these instances both the Harvard course and parts of the Open Admissions movement focused on standards, especially on how academic standards could be maintained despite the widely different social standing of the new students.

Open admissions Guideline 3 (about standards) then conflicts with Guideline 4 (about ethnic integration). Guideline 3 aims to maintain the status quo by asserting existing (though not named) standards. In this way, it is separated from the historical change of Open Admission. Ahistorical claims of value serve dominant and conserving views of language standards. Barbara Herrnstein Smith's exploration of the political workings of transcendent assertions of value in *Contingencies of Value*, cited in Chapter 1, further explains how "standards" work against "ethnic integration":

> when someone or some group of people insist(s) on the *objective* necessity or propriety of their own social, political, or moral judgments and actions, and deny the *contingency* of the conditions and perspectives from which those judgments and actions proceed, it must be—and always is—a move to assign dominant status to the *particular* conditions and perspectives . . . ; it must be—and always is—simultaneously a move to deny the existence and relevance, and to suppress the claims, of *other* conditions and perspectives. (1988, 181)

Under this analysis, we can see why Guideline 3 appears to be so in conflict with "ethnic integration." Open Admissions students entered City College with perspectives, language, and education that seemed to differ wildly from those of their professors. Guideline number 3 denied the existence of these "other conditions and perspectives."

This sense of standards is ironic because it directly conflicts with a principle reason why Open Admissions was initiated: the profound distrust of standardized measures of performance. One of the central arguments for Open Admissions was that standardized measures, such as the SAT, were racist. The eloquent and successful arguments against standardized tests and grades in the late 1960s and early 1970s challenge the idea that any progress toward socially progressive assessment has been made in the last twenty years. Open Admissions was possible because, during a brief window of generosity, university officials let go of the dominance of that singular plural sense of standards that Williams referred to, and they allowed students to enter, trusting both the students and the university to engage in education. But only until students entered college where "standards" in the singular plural re-emerged. University officials seemed to believe that the student body could change without really changing the university. The success of Open Admissions was limited by the inability or reluctance to think of standards as an ordinary plural that changes with social conditions and with people who develop and hold them.

When standards were discussed, these standards inevitably referred to writing ability. It is not obvious that this should be the case. I imagine that Open Admissions students entered City College with widely varying academic preparation, some of them probably knew very little academic math, some may have known very little science or the kind of history that is taught in college. But accounts of Open Admissions rarely focus on these subject matters as evidence of declining standards. Instead, charges of student illiteracy flew. Literacy issues provided critics with a "double-whammy" because of the particular association of literacy with values. Not only were students lacking in knowledge or skill, they were nearly immoral, too. To shout with urgency that students don't know science is to argue for science education, to claim that students are illiterate is to argue that they are *unfit* for college. Literacy studies in the last ten years have effectively demonstrated that what gets called illiterate is historically and socially contingent and that the charge of illiteracy carries with it a potent charge of moral unfitness.

One of Open Admission's most notorious critics, L. G. Heller, author of *The Death of the American University: With Special Reference to the Collapse of City College of New York*, charged that Open Admissions was the result of the collaboration of powerful student radicals (often African American) and weak administrators. The result, in Heller's view, was declining standards and the death of the university. Although his arguments are wide-ranging, many of them center on the issue of standards. He rails against the falling standards, calling Open Admissions "a political device for giving a college diploma without giving a college education." He calls one of his students "virtually illiterate" and suggests that average students "shine" in Open Admissions in "comparison with their nearly illiterate classmates" (1973, 93). Heller's views were loud enough to attract the attention of Robert Evans and Robert Novak who published a national column that began with this anecdote: "Utterly baffled by the profundities of first-year history at City College, a newly enrolled freshman this fall told his professor he simply could not make sense out of his textbook 'because too many words are just too long'" (quoted in Heller 1973, 81). Evans and Novak go on to ask, "Is the enormous expense of higher education the best way to care for semi-literate high school graduates who might otherwise drift into crime? And is the high price of drastically lowered academic standards really necessary to achieve this goal?" (in Heller 1973, 81). The theme was even picked up by Vice President Spiro Agnew who crisscrossed the country accusing City College of giving out "bargain basement diplomas." Note Evans and Novak's persistent attention to literacy standards, attention that calls into question the validity of the Guideline 4 of Open Admissions by calling Open Admissions students (most of whom were students of color) "semi-literate high school graduates who might otherwise drift into crime." In a clause, there it is, the connection of literacy standards with morality, and a stark example of how writing standards were used to argue against the entrance of students of color into City College.

Theodore Gross' book, *Academic Turmoil*, echoes some of Heller's themes, though less hysterically and more moderately. Gross' understanding of writing standards shows how standards worked, as a singular plural, against the success of Open Admissions. Like Heller, he argues that faculty and administrators failed to uphold standards: "At the moment when standards had to be perpetuated, they were relaxed" (1980, 4). He characterizes students as suffering from "deep linguistic shortcomings" (22), as having a "weak command of the language," and needing "to master the writing of English." He argues against CCCC's document, the "Students' Right to Their Own Language," by stating that "most writing is exposition and exposition is standardized" (22).

Many of the complaints about standards in Open Admissions and elsewhere are cast in terms that claim dominance through objectivity. When Gross talks about the "weak command of the language," or "the writing of English," the definite article marks his argument, as does the passive construction in "exposition is standardized." The most specific that Gross gets about the "deep linguistic shortcomings" is: "The greatest task among many blacks seemed to be that of verb tense." And he really doesn't even mean "tense"; he means verb endings.

Clearly many teachers worked hard under difficult conditions with little or no education in teaching composition. Gross himself points out how deeply underprepared the teachers of Open Admissions were. He hired twenty-one basic writing teachers in one year, almost all of them Ph.D. candidates in literature from Columbia or NYU. Their measure of "writing" was shaped by the belief that their literary training prepared them to know "the quality of superb writing and thought against which other writing and thought could be measured" (1980, 37). Yet Gross notes—with insight and some anger—that training in literature at Columbia, for instance, included no ethnic authors and no pedagogical training at all.

Gross' memoirs paint a microcosmic picture of the way standards were handled; his story is a tangle of competing ideologies. Like the university itself, he was conflicted. He attempted to respond to social conditions that required changing standards. At one point in his argument he pleads for the faculty "to stop judging our students and start understanding them" (20). Yet at other times he saw falling standards as evidence of the decline and fall of the traditional humanities. Against threat of massive demographic change at City College, the institutional response was both to accept (because of the pressure from people of color) and contain.

The strategies of containment include both institutional separation and ideological distancing. Into these tangles of ideologies and social forces emerged one of the most influential scholars in composition studies, Mina Shaughnessy, whose *Errors and Expectations* is a brilliant political document, one from which both conservatives like E.D. Hirsch and Thomas Farrell and progressives like Patricia Bizzell and David Bartholomae find inspiration. Gross retells a story that indicates the degree to which Shaughnessy's achievement (perhaps more outside City College than inside) was aligned with Open Admissions. According to Gross, in summer of 1978, the Rockefeller Foundation organized a retrospective on Open Admissions; the opening talk called Open Admissions a "flat failure." The most significant response (again, according to Gross) was from Benjamin DeMott, who said, " 'Well, there has been a significant amount of good. . . . For one thing, we have Professor Shaughnessy's book' " (Gross 1980, 140–41).

The status of this achievement is still being argued. I'll argue that Shaughnessy's book embodied *and still embodies*, in an unsurprising way, the tensions of access and exclusion. Her achievement is the reconsideration of what we now call "basic writer" (a term that has often has been used as a euphemism for African Americans [Jones 1993]). She reconceived of the errors that basic writers made, and she unequivocally asserted the intelligence of those errors. For 1977 standards, then, she asserted a theory of difference in place of a theory of deficit—at least in part. To speak of the "logic" of error removed error from the semantic domains of laziness or uncleanliness, and it removed those students from the moral judgments about literacy like the ones Evans and Novak make.

This generous attitude toward students is what seems to have given Shaughnessy a nearly unassailable position in our profession, for it was only recently, nearly fifteen years after the publication of *Errors and Expectations*, that critiques of her work began to emerge. The first major critique was not well received, nor is it much cited, despite its anticipation of many of the issues that composition faced in the 1980s and 1990s. John Rouse's 1979 critique of Shaughnessy, "The Politics of Composition," anticipates many current critiques (Bartholomae, "The Tidy House," Lu, "Redefining," Horner, "Mapping Errors and Expectations"), especially critiquing the formalist stance toward language as being politically conservative. In doing so, Rouse shows how, in addition to the stance of acceptance, Shaughnessy's work also embodied a stance of containment, a way of indoctrinating students by focusing on grammatical "rules." This aspect of Shaughnessy has been suppressed by representations of her work by Bartholomae, Lyons, and others. And yet, rereading *Errors and Expectations,* one is struck by the microscopic attention to form, and except for Chapter 7, all of it to levels of discourse smaller than the sentence. In one sense this close reading is what Shaughnessy is admired for, and what Bartholomae and others have learned from her example. Student writing deserves the same kind of close attention that literature does. And yet, this close attention is not only a tool of analysis, but a justification for the worst kind of writing pedagogy: acontextual worksheets on grammar and usage. Even in 1977, this kind of pedagogy was not acceptable (although it was practiced then and is still practiced now).

Shaughnessy, however, created a space called "Basic Writing" wherein the rules of writing process pedagogy could be broken. She did this by claiming an exaggerated sense of difference for basic writers and the field of basic writing. As Bruce Horner points out in "Mapping Errors and Expectations for Basic Writing," Shaughnessy relied on three metaphors, "Beginners," "Foreigners," and "Frontier" to describe basic writing. These metaphors, from Shaughnessy's point of view, replaced worse descriptions of basic writers: lazy, ignorant, incapable. Yet these new metaphors were not neutral replacements, as Horner points out. "Beginner" calls to mind explanations of basic writers as cognitively or ethically immature, much as the early work of Andrea Lunsford, Patricia Bizzell, or Janice Hayes. "Foreigner" confounds the issue by forcing a metaphor of "other" on native New Yorkers. Additionally, "foreigner" leads us into thinking about teaching "in terms of conversion or deracination" (Horner 1994, 35–36), unpleasant alternatives both. Finally the "frontier" metaphor was first challenged by Rouse who saw Shaughnessy's use of it as a way of differentiating the teaching of basic writing from the teaching of "regular" writing and thus ignoring the gains in theory and practice of the 1970s. Horner also calls attention to the connections between "foreigner" and "frontier." Foreigners in Shaughnessy's use are

> natives who nonetheless belong to another country, members of a culture and a community who are yet nonmembers, knowledgeable youth incapable of communication, "aliens in their own culture, strangers in their own land." (Horner 1994, 35)

These descriptions bring to mind for Horner the American frontier experience where "not everyone was a stranger but the strangers, with considerable firepower, on encountering native inhabitants of the territory, decided the natives were the strangers, "true outsiders," "out-landish," or "foreign" (Horner 1994, 35). This metaphor limits the role of education for basic writers.

Rouse, in his reply to Gerald Graff's defensive response to his article, calls Shaughnessy's achievements "a great political accomplishment, satisfying and reassuring all the factions involved" (1979, 871). What Shaughnessy was able to do, which *was* a remarkable political accomplishment, was to save an institutional structure of writing—invented by the Harvard course—that was deeply challenged by the entrance of large numbers of African American and Puerto Rican students. She was a liberal and satisfied liberal desires by unequivocally believing that Open Admissions students were "educable." Yet her pedagogy retained a program of "winnowing and indoctrinating" that served to contain challenges to the curriculum or challenges to prevailing notions of literacy. For African American students already aware of institutional opposition to their presence, a writing program based on any of the three central metaphors in Shaughnessy's program resulted in continued marginalization.

In the years following the publication of Shaughnessy's book, basic writing programs continue to be limited by narrow definitions that misrepresent the languages and communities of their students. Virtually all of the labels for basic writers are inaccurate in one way or another. "Remedial," as Mike Rose has shown, implies metaphorically that the writer has a "disease" or a "mental defect" (1985, 349). "Developmental" suggests that the writer is young or immature. And "basic," the term I reluctantly use, implies that these writers are simple or stuck on some rudimentary level. More recent social explorations into discourse communities have seen basic writers as "initiates" into the foreign world of academic discourse. But these social theories also underestimate and misrepresent the discourse communities of basic writers. Drawing from John Ogbu's work on African Americans' education, I propose redefining what people call basic writing rhetorically, not developmentally, as acts that negotiate the complex cultural situations of student of color in majority-dominated institutions. This redefinition supports the curricular and pedagogical changes argued for in Chapters 4 and 5, including the elimination of no-credit basic writing programs.

Institutional Failures

Most teachers have student skeletons in their mental closet, those students whom we have a sense that we disserved, those whom we failed even though we knew we misunderstood them. One of mine is Monica, a student I tutored in our basic writing program. Her steadfast refusal to engage the basic writing curriculum has helped me think through the way that the work of basic writing programs is affected by more than just curriculum, but by institutional ideologies of writing instruction held by teachers and students. At the time I was coordinator of the basic writing program and in charge of training the adjunct tutors that accompanied the program. I decided it was necessary for me to do what I was training the tutors to do, so one semester I tutored for a basic writing course and met once a week with a group of four students, one of whom was Monica.

Monica didn't talk much, a habit that made me uncomfortable. She wore her sunglasses even in the tutoring session. She was upfront about not wanting to take this course, or any other course that would interfere with her goal of becoming a nurse. She didn't think a writing course, particularly this no-credit remedial course, was going to help her at all. I recall asking her about literacy practices in the nursing field, and while she was aware of the kinds and amount of writing that nurses do, she didn't think that basic writing was going to help her.

The course was taught by a good graduate student teacher who created a course that explored the various ways that people educate themselves. Among the readings were J. D. Salinger's *The Catcher in the Rye*, Richard Rodriguez's *The Hunger of Memory*, and Frederick Douglass' autobiography. The teacher sought to give basic writers intellectually challenging readings, whole texts, and a variety of assignments culminating in a research paper on the student's own career goals. Monica did most of the assignments, but usually perfunctorily. One assignment— on how family traditions teach us—was long and detailed. It was about Thanksgiving and described the preparation of food and the washing of dishes. There is not much on what she learned or on the significance of the event for her. She didn't do most of the reading. She missed class fourteen times. She read *The Catcher in the Rye*, and perhaps Frederick Douglass, but she did not read *The Hunger of Memory*. She was the only woman in our tutoring group, and one of three African Americans. To give a sense of her typical rhetorical stance (both in speaking and writing), here is an excerpt from an interview done as a prewriting exercise to a paper on her own education. She is being interviewed by one of the other students, Adam, although all students and the tutor (me) are present:

Adam: Why are you in the process of obtaining a college education?

Monica: Because I wanted to be a nurse and in order to be a nurse you have to go to college.

Adam: Are you a junior, freshman, sophomore?

Monica: Freshman.

Adam: What kind of nurse do you want to be?

Monica: Administrative nurse.

Adam: What kind of courses will help you the most?

Monica: Biology, chemistry, human anatomy.

Adam: What made you want to become a nurse?

Monica: I just like to help people who are sick.

Adam: What do you think about Rodriguez?

Monica: To tell you the truth I didn't read the book. I wrote the paper though.

Adam: What do you think about Caulfield?

Monica: He's smart in a way, but in a way he's not. He kept doing things over and over again. It's like he don't look at the world as it is. He just looks at it in his own way and I guess he expects the world to just go his own way.

Adam: What kind of attitude do you need to be a nurse?

Monica: Um, a positive attitude.

Adam: Do you think Caulfield could make a good nurse?

Monica: No.

Tom: Good question.

Adam: So what things were right and wrong in your educational career?

Monica: Uh, I really don't know. Everything went fine.

Adam: You didn't have no problem in P. E. classes?

Monica: No.

Adam: Your friends weren't dancing in the halls?

Monica: Yes, they were dancing in the halls.

Adam is a great interviewer, but he really doesn't get anywhere. It's obvious that Monica is capable—her answer about Holden Caulfield, while not developed, is interesting. But mostly, Monica is not buying into this exercise. She doesn't want to talk about what's been good or bad in her educational history or what makes a good nurse. She doesn't even respond to Adam's question about dancing in the halls, although it's a brief connection between two who know what it means to be dancing in the halls.

Monica's own summary of her participation in the class near the end of the semester confirms my sense of her nonengagement:

> My experience in this class was very motivated and interesting. In the beginning of the course it seemed like it would be fun to be here. Maybe, if the class was at a later time I would have enjoyed it better than I did.

This course was graded credit/no credit and the teacher and I were both concerned that Monica would receive a no credit. The teacher spoke to her about absences and late papers and agreed that the final paper would have to be in on time and be excellent in order for Monica to receive credit. The final paper asked students to research their own career choices, visit the workplace if applicable, interview practicing members of that profession, and tell about their reasons for wanting to join this profession.

Monica's final paper was not what the teacher expected or wanted. Much of it is copied verbatim from the description of the nursing major from our university catalog, including the number of units required for graduation, the sequence of courses, general education requirements. She included, without explanation, a description of "The Certificate in Public Health Nursing," which is a program for students who already have a bachelor's degree, a program not applicable to Monica's situation. Monica typed and spaced her paper exactly like the catalog.

There is a brief window into Monica's motives for becoming a nurse in this paper. After the capital letter "B," signifying part two of the assigned duties of the initial assignment, Monica wrote the following:

> I made the decision about fourteen years ago, and I promised my deceased mother that I would become a nurse to help the sick people. The reason why I decided to become nurse was because my mother was a diabetic, and I didn't like to see her give herself insulin everyday and dropping pills in this tube to see if her sugar level was average.

The section following this paragraph consists of an interview with an unnamed, retired nurse's aide. The interview is reminiscent of Adam and Monica's discussion, short, without a lot of useful information. The interview concludes with Monica asking, "What kind of advice would you give me?" The answer is, "Study hard, be all you can be. Always look to bigger and better things."

The teacher did not pass her, and I, though puzzled by Monica's final paper, supported that decision. But what did this paper mean? The easy answer is that Monica thought the class was meaningless and tried to do as little as possible and still pass. This explanation doesn't satisfy, however. Although copying the catalog may have been easier than writing about nursing, it isn't much easier, especially because she reproduced even the spacing, the format, of the catalog.

Her reproduction, however, was not exact. The section in the catalog entitled "Literacy Requirements" was rewritten slightly. She summarized the upper division writing requirement and then underlined the following: "Students are required to be certified by the end of Semester IV; failure to do so will result in dismissal from the program." This underlined section, of course, refers to the problem of passing the no-credit basic writing course in a timely fashion, a course she was in danger of failing.

It is tempting, given the history of this course, to see Monica's action as a heroic gesture of resistance, like Pierre Menard rewriting *Don*

Quixote in the well-known Borges story. Instead, I want to reread her act in light of the history of freshman composition courses, and the basic writing courses that developed from them, as discussed in Chapter 2.

As an institutional structure, basic writing intensifies the "institutionalized ambiguity" of freshman composition (Russell 1992). Even more than freshman composition, basic writing is concerned with issues of access. Its history as a part of the Open Admission movement at City College attests to basic writing's commitment to what we now call students of color. And yet with this commitment comes an equally powerful commitment to the second half of composition's "institutionalized ambiguity"—the part about gatekeeping. Basic writers have been institutionally positioned even more precariously than first-year writers. As no-credit courses on the periphery of the curriculum, as courses designed as college prep, they exist in an academic limbo.

The justification for this tenuous and marginalized institutional position is that these writers are supposedly doing high school work. The definition of basic writing as "remedial" relies on what Mike Rose calls the myth of transience when it calls upon the universities to do the work that high schools have failed to do, but only to take it on provisionally, not as a part of our real curriculum. Never mind the historical fact that high schools have never done this work, and that colleges and universities have been singing this tune at least since 1841, when the president of Brown University complained about the underpreparedness of his entering freshmen (Rose 1989, 5).

This provisional nature of the institutional commitment to basic writing has made it the domain of part-time faculty, programs of developmental studies, stepchildren of learning skills programs. Often basic writing programs have no departmental base, and even when they do, the sense that they are of less importance than freshman composition, which is less important than literature studies, gives them very little intellectual status. Students perceive this.

For students like Monica, for whom the whole composition requirement is an unexplained punishment, the basic writing course is doubly punitive, for it bears no baccalaureate credit. It is a course that hassles her on her way to do the real work of her university education. This sense of being hassled derives from three connected ideologies— deficit theories, skills instruction, and service goals—stemming from the institutional histories of these programs.

The first of these, deficit theory, was the topic of a session at the 1988 National Council of Teachers of English annual meeting on "The Reemergence of Deficit Theories." The panelists—Geneva Smitherman, Jacqueline Jones Royster, and Barbara M. Flores—all noted that deficit theories tend to go underground, then resurface in new forms. The point of the panel was that while deficit theories, those theories of language learning that presume ignorance and inability in students and children, may change terms, the ideas are the same and the students who most suffer from the pedagogy that springs from it are the same: speakers of nonstandard dialect, almost always African Americans. Deficit theories have been around a long time—before Martin Deustch and Bereiter and Englemann—and no doubt they'll be around as long as racism and sexism and classism affect education. Certainly deficit theories have influenced the shape of basic writing programs. Consider, for instance, the documents that officially shape higher education basic writing programs in the state of California, including the program at California State University, Chico, where Monica was enrolled. The Master Plan Renewed (1987), a state publication that shapes policy for all segments of higher education in California, defines the students in the basic writing program as: "Students who are nearly college ready, but exhibit serious multiple skill deficiencies that require instruction at two levels below the Freshman level in English." Deficit theory, at least in higher education in California, seems never to have gone underground at all and remains the official policy.

In addition to defining students by their deficiencies, deficit theories—especially in their application to basic writers—tend to reduce writing to a set of discrete skills to be learned, especially the countable ones such as punctuation and spelling. Workbooks and grammar modules still populate basic writing workshops and computer work stations from the mistaken idea that students need to develop "basic skills," skills that they almost always already possess. Any approach that separates language features from intention and meaning for the purpose of "practice" is a skills approach. Richard Ohmann has explored the ideological consequences of teaching style as a skill in "Use Definite, Specific, Concrete Language." Ohmann's essay shows how the stylistic advice of textbooks, by transforming style to a set of skills (use definite, specific, concrete language), separates style from questions of meaning, intention, and especially action. Instead, the textbooks "push the student writer always toward the language that most nearly reproduces the immediate experience and away from language that might be used to understand it, transform it, and relate it to everything else" (1987, 250). The consequence for students is that when we teach "a skill like this we may inadvertently suggest to students that they be less inquiring and less intelligent than they are capable of being" (1987, 242). Students, particularly in basic writing courses, internalize the skills approach and claim it as their goal for the course. Monica, for instance, wrote the following summary of her writing at the beginning of the semester:

> As a writer I tend to become very detailed about my subjects or the items I have described; that's a strength in my writing. But, as a weakness I tend to leave out words, the key words. Punctuation is alright

> sometimes. . . . My hopes for [basic writing] is to improve my writing, by writing complete sentences.

My experience with students' statements about their own writing is that they almost always write about skills, and they almost always write inaccurately about them. I didn't see evidence that Monica left out words in her writing, nor were complete sentences a particular problem for her. Her goals for the class and thus her construction of its purpose, reflect the unimaginative and politically ambiguous nature of the course. She saw her writing as a set of techniques, not a product of culture. Authors from the less overtly political Frank Smith to the overtly political Stanley Aronowitz and Henry Giroux have demonstrated how teaching basic skills underestimates and undermines both teachers and students.

Mike Rose's "The Language of Exclusion" explores how writing as "skill" works in the university, showing how the focus on skills has reduced the teaching of writing and the discipline of writing to a "second-class intellectual status." The skills view of writing instruction grew from a particular historical context—early twentieth century's stress on efficiency and utilitarianism—and led teachers to concentrate mostly on "mechanical/grammatical" features at the expense of "rhetorical/conceptual" dimensions. Rose makes clear that this history is still with us, as we have "writing skills hierarchies, writing skills assessments, and writing skills centers" (1985, 346). He is also clear about the problems with this approach:

> . . . such work is built on a set of highly questionable assumptions: that a writer has a relatively fixed repository of linguistic blunders that can be pinpointed and then corrected through drill, that repetitive drill on specific linguistic features represented in isolated sentences will result in mastery of linguistic (or stylistic or rhetorical) principles, that bits of discourse bereft of rhetoric or conceptual context can form the basis of curriculum and assessment, that good writing is correct writing, and that correctness has to do with pronoun choice, verb forms, and the like. (1985, 345)

The definition of writing as skill leads to a diminished and specialized role for writing in the university curriculum: the service course, another set of ideas that prevents a more generous understanding of basic writing. Writing courses are the best known and purest example of a service course. While other general education courses—math, critical thinking, and occasionally speech courses—are designed as courses that "serve" the university as a whole, most of these courses also introduce students to disciplines. Because writing courses are housed either in English departments usually dominated by literature faculty or in no department at all (many writing courses are part of a "program"), they often lose the connection with a discipline and field of inquiry and the professional authority that comes with that connection. This is especially true of basic writing programs, which are sometimes housed outside the English department even when the rest of the writing courses are taught within the department. The university conceives of these courses as devoid of content, teaching only a set of neutral tools.

The role of such courses is "service" and the obligation of the curriculum is to benefit all the other content areas. Such a role often leaves curricular decisions in the hands of those who are not especially knowledgeable about writing instruction and removes curricular responsibility from the teacher. In the absence of this connection with content, basic writing "content" becomes a matter of bureaucratic concern. Devoid of content, these writing courses become better suited to the general task of social sorting. If basic writing programs primarily concern themselves with serving the university, then political questions, or any questions that challenge existing definitions of basic writing, become irrelevant to the bureaucratic task of reproducing the program.

Monica's opinion that this course was irrelevant to her career goals was based on the service assumption that it was *supposed* to be directly relevant to any major in the university. This version of the universal writing course, embedded in its history at Harvard and elsewhere, makes claims to a privileged place in the general education curriculum based on promises that it (the course) cannot keep. In other words, Monica correctly perceived the limited transferability of composition, a conclusion supported by a great deal of research. For instance, in a collaborative study at the University of Utah, five students set out to explore just how their first year writing course helped them in their other courses. In light of Monica's assertions, their conclusions are relevant: "The 'discourse community' defined in composition was rarely reproduced later because students and teachers in other introductory-level courses operated in two very separate and often conflicting rhetorical worlds" (Anderson et al. 1990, 11). Similarly, Judith Rodby, in "(Con)-Testing Ideas of Literacy (or There Are No Basics in This Class)" argues that literacy does not come in levels. Using evidence from literacy studies and cognitive science, Rodby show that literacy is "not a static 'thing' but rather it is a practice, a set of socially organized activities" (1995, 11). Her conclusion is that basic writing courses create basic writers, and do little to "prepare" students for a different context. This conclusion challenges the very definition of "preparatory" and service, the ideological underpinnings of basic writing.

This bundle of interconnected ideologies—deficit theory, skills instruction, and service—has dislocated the authority of both the teacher of basic writing and the student. Teachers of basic writing, as Rose points out, are frequently nontenure-track staff and are institutionally less secure. What to teach is usually decided by a program coordinator who may or may not be educated in the teaching of writing. Set syllabi and required textbooks leave little choice for the teacher and little inspiration for the students. Students, more often than not, are not given baccalaureate credit for the course and consequently the course may feel like a punitive experience. The curriculum in basic writing—with important exceptions—has lagged behind the enormous changes in writing instruction. All too often it remains focused on grammatical conventions.

The influence of these ideologies on writing instruction, added to the fact that basic writing programs typically enroll a high percentage of students of color and working-class students, gives basic writing programs the potential to work oppressively, against access. The students who have historically been excluded from university education are too often taught an outmoded, limiting curriculum based on outdated assumptions. Many basic writing teachers, like their students, are denied the intellectual support to enliven their jobs. They have little control over their curriculum and teach in institutional settings that inhibit thoughtful considerations of their course and their students.

Monica was not enrolled in a skills course. Her basic writing curriculum aimed to "encourage full expression of past voices and experimentation with new ones, including academic voices" (Voorhees 1989, 14). The difficulty, however, was that Monica's own idea of the course as a skills course was supported by the no-credit institutional position. Additionally, even if she believed that the course was not a skills course, a course that encouraged "experimentation with new voices" may have seemed equally irrelevant to her career in nursing. So the course seemed not only to refuse to help her with her skills, it did not even attempt to fulfill a service role. The pedagogy therefore was not only limited by its institutional position, but also by ideologies that shaped the way students were able to perceive the course. Monica's failure then, could be seen as an institutional failure, but one that was overdetermined. Conflicting expectations (such as a progressive curriculum in a no-credit course), many of them reflected in institutional structures, produced an uninterpretable gap between Monica and the curriculum. In this light, Monica's skeptical refusal to engage with the course seems like an understandable and logical lack of trust.

Initiation Theories

While the ideologies of deficit theories, skills instruction, and service courses refuse to be dislodged easily from the academy, what many have seen as "the social turn" in composition studies influenced basic writing, too. Particularly in the work of David Bartholomae and Patricia Bizzell, we find definitions of basic writing that focus on social group membership and the exploration of discourse communities. This work, influenced by anthropologists' understanding of culture and community, defines the basic writer as an "initiate" into the academic community. While initiation theories have been helpful in shaping curriculum and in defining basic writers, early formulations simplified both the academic community and the students' communities, representing both as homogeneous and mutually exclusive. Pedagogies based on these early formulations shared common purposes with service courses; they taught the students what they did not know so that they would fit into the university.

Despite this understanding of community, the two major statements of initiation theory, David Bartholomae's "Inventing the University" and Patricia Bizzell's "What Happens When Basic Writers Come to College?" are helpful in many respects; they ask basic writing teachers and researchers to reconceive their work in the social and political terms that give dignity to their own and their students' efforts. Bartholomae, for instance, challenges writing researchers (and that includes all teachers) to "conceive of a writer as at work within a text and simultaneously, then, within a society, a history, and a culture" (1984, 162). I would like to explore these two articles, in part because they continue to influence our definitions of basic writing, and in part because they best represent "initiation theory." I should reiterate that both Bartholomae and Bizzell have eloquently reconsidered their own assumptions, showing both how unified understandings of academic discourse are oppressive, and how pedagogies based simply on initiation may not work in the interests of oppressed students.

The central argument in "Inventing the University" is that basic writers' unfamiliarity with academic discourse causes them to "approximate" the language of the academy without really knowing its discourse conventions, and that this "approximate discourse" is a necessary step in the initiation process:

> What our beginning students need to learn is to extend themselves, by successive approximations, into the commonplaces, set phrases, rituals and gestures, habits of mind, tricks of persuasion, obligatory conclusions and necessary connections that determine the "what might be said" and constitute knowledge within the various branches of our academic community. (1984, 146)

This process is necessary only because of assumptions Bartholomae makes about the relationship between the students' discourse community and the academy's. First, Bartholomae presents the two communities as distinct and separate, focusing on how the academy's discourse is very different from the students'. Throughout "Inventing the University" Bartholomae describes the academy as having "peculiar" ways of knowing, "specialized" discourse, giving the impression of a large distance between what students know and all they need to know. Secondly, Bartholomae assumes that the academic discourse community is basically stable while the students' discourse is dynamic. Students are initiated into, but do not change, the academic community.

Bizzell, too, in "What Happens," shares these assumptions. She describes the discourse gap in terms of "world view":

> . . . basic writers, upon entering the academic community, are being asked to learn a new dialect and new discourse conventions, but the outcome of such learning is acquisition of a whole new world view. Their difficulties, then, are best understood as stemming from the initial distance between their world views and the academic world view. (1986, 297)

The gap is signified by the "whole new world view" that basic writers must acquire. Both Bizzell and Bartholomae are sensitive to the costs of this change, the sense of loss that many students might feel in abandoning their worldview. Bizzell, for instance, states that basic writers learn the conflict of worldviews "immediately and forcefully when they come to college . . . , when they experience the distance between their home dialects and Standard English and the debilitating unfamiliarity they feel with academic ways of shaping thought in discourse" (1986, 300). Like Bartholomae, Bizzell presents the academy as essentially stable; students will change for it, but not the other way around. Both articles suggest that because of the power and value of the academic worldview, the change, and its attendant losses, will be worth it.

Let me consider the central assumptions of the initiation argument: first, the distance between students' discourse and academic discourse. Bartholomae bases his argument in "Inventing the University" on his examination of freshman placement tests. In these kinds of timed tests students believe that they must do something called "college-level" writing, perhaps for the first time. Students who are most socially uncomfortable with the university tend to exaggerate the newness and difference of "college-level." These exams test both writing ability in a timed-test context and the degree of comfort and authority that students feel in such circumstances. This second fact may be the reason for the higher representation of socially marginalized students in basic writing programs. Bartholomae, however, privileges textual evidence, assuming that the timed tests can reveal, among other things, basic writers' "native arguments." But the discomfort that he so eloquently writes about may stem less from basic writers' ignorance of the academy's discourse conventions than from a fear that their own resources of discourse may be irrelevant or damaging to their success in college.

Certainly, Bartholomae's analysis fits with the experiences basic writing teachers have with their students, especially in the first weeks of class. Students are sincerely uncertain, frequently guessing and misguessing what the academic game will be like. What makes me uncomfortable about Bartholomae's argument is that he turns a helpful and critical analysis of a situation into a pedagogy. Basic writing students, because of their social insecurities, may be exaggerating their "outlandishness" and underestimating the relevance and validity of their own discourse community to work in the academy. To teach the distinctiveness of academic discourse, its separation from student literacy, perpetuates the cultural divisions and conflicts that cause the discomfort of many of our students. By overstating the difference between academic discourse and students' discourse, especially to attribute what differences there are to linguistic habits or cognitive conventions, we send a message to those who are most uncomfortable, most anxious, about the status of their language in the university (African Americans, Latinos, nonnative speakers): We write a different "English" here, forget what you know. Students in this situation must feel like they are facing a linguistic abyss. The language with which they are familiar is an interference; they must abandon it.

In addition to underestimating the students' own discourse community and its relevance to academic work, the initiation argument also exaggerates the stability and coherence of the discourse of the academy. Both Bartholomae and Bizzell have articulated concerns about the initiation model in the last several years. Bizzell has been particularly frank and insightful about her earlier work. For instance, in "Arguing About Literacy," she states that understanding academic literacy as "monolithic is misleading, and itself politically oppressive" (1988, 141). In many ways, she has led explorations that go beyond initiation theory. Joseph Harris, in "The Idea of Community in the Study of Writing," supports Bizzell's later speculations on community by arguing that all discourse communities are varied:

> There has been much debate in recent years over whether we need, above all, to respect our students' "right to their own language," or to teach them the ways and forms of "academic discourse." Both sides of this argument, in the end, rest their cases on the same suspect generalization: that we and our students belong to different and fairly distinct communities of discourse, that we have "our" "academic" discourse and they have "their own" "common" (?!) ones. The choice is one between opposing fictions. The "languages" that our students bring to us cannot but have been shaped, at least in part, by their ex-

periences in school, and thus must, in some ways, already be "academic." Similarly, our teaching will and should always be affected by a host of beliefs and values that we hold regardless of our roles as academics. What we see in the classroom, then, are not two coherent and competing discourses but many overlapping and conflicting ones. (1989, 18–19)

Once academic discourse is understood as "overlapping and conflicting," its dominance is less total. The requirement to join it thus requires students to give up much less; total deracination isn't necessary. Giroux argues for a definition of educational institutions that supports Harris' sense of the polyvocal nature of the academic discourse community. Giroux critiques reproductive theories of education, arguing that they have misconceived of schools as only institutions of domination and reproduction, as uniform "factories of oppression" reproducing dominant culture. Giroux objects to this analysis of schools, mainly because it omits the possibility of agency for working-class students, the possibility and existence of resistance. This resistance is documented by ethnographic studies of education such as Paul Willis' *Learning to Labor*. And what this resistance shows is that schools are "contested," reproducing "the larger society while containing spaces to resist its dominating logic" (Giroux 1988, xxxiii). As such, the academic discourse community isn't a complete or unified community to be initiated into. It already contains portions of the discourses that students, even basic writers, bring with them.

Basic writing teachers' experiences with two groups of students, nonnative speakers and speakers of Black Vernacular English, would seem to argue against the claim that students' language is not significantly different from academic discourse. The claim, of course, rests on the word "significantly." No doubt the language of basic writers differs from academic discourse (no matter how we define it). But the pedagogy of initiation may make it more difficult for basic writers to succeed. They not only have to master "skills" (as in the service courses), but they have to acquire a new way of understanding, knowing, arguing, reflecting.

The Clash of Cultural Styles

The distinctiveness of discourse communities, as an explanation for basic writing, has a parallel in the work of educational theorists trying to explain why education has failed to reach African American students. This body of work focuses on how cultural difference interferes with communication, especially classroom talk. While this work brings cultural conflicts into focus, these conflicts are presented without a strong sense of the history that produced them. A magnificent analysis of this "clash of cultural styles" is Shirley Brice Heath's (1983) *Ways with Words*. Heath spent ten years living with and studying two communities in the Piedmont area of the Carolinas, one white, which she called "Roadville," and one black, which she called "Trackton." Heath shows, in fascinating detail, how the language learning styles of these communities differ, yet how neither community's style of language use fits well with the "mainstream" culture of school. With regards to African American students, Heath shows how Trackton children see language as "performance": playful, inventive, designed to entertain. Although rich and complex, this view of language isn't understood well or appreciated by mainstream teachers. Consequently, students from Trackton don't do well in school.

A similar, more specific example of the "clash of cultural styles" explanation comes from Sarah Michael's chapter in *Social Construction of Literacy*, where Michaels examines the response of a teacher to an African American student's narrative. Deena, the black student, narrates in what Michaels calls a "topic associating" style, which, according to Michaels, is typical of African American speakers. In a topic-associating style, narratives consist "of a series of segments or episodes that are implicitly linked in highlighting some person or theme" (1986, 103). This style clashes with a "topic-centered" style, preferred by the teacher and by white students. So when Deena takes her turn in "sharing time," the teacher believes that Deena has difficulty planning in advance and sticking to one idea. Consequently, she interrupts Deena's story with what Deena considers inappropriate and irrelevant questions, confusing and angering Deena and compounding the teacher's sense that Deena can't focus.

Solutions to the "clash of cultural style" explanation usually involve new consciousness on the part of the teacher, rather than attending to larger social and political changes. In Deena's case, the researcher spoke with the teacher about a topic-associating style as a legitimate way of constructing narratives. The teacher, Michaels reports, subsequently dealt with the perceived lack of coherence in the narratives in a very different way. Instead of assuming incoherence, she asked the children to explain the connections, which she now knew were there. Similarly, in Heath's study, the teachers learned about different language styles and gained consciousness of their own ethnocentricity (1983, 270). Both studies assume well-meaning people on both sides of the cultural clash who can step easily out of their historical roles. They pay little attention to the meaning of the stylistic difference and pay more attention to the existence of the difference. "Misunderstandings" among well-meaning teachers and students cause poor performances in school.

These explanations, moreover, underestimate the historical and social facts of marginalization and oppression, just as Bartholomae's and Bizzell's conceptions of students' discourse communities too tightly circumscribe basic writers' worlds. Bartholomae and Bizzell carefully consider issues of power and authority, although I believe their early explorations of discourse communities underestimate the students' power to resist. Michaels and Heath, while more specific about the nature of cultural difference, leave unexamined the difference in the power and authority on the two sides of the clash, and thus their studies do not stress enough the historical nature of this difference. Even though the research for *Ways with Words* was motivated by court-mandated desegregation, and even though it compares a black community with a white community, Heath's book ignores issues of racism and even warns readers away from considering such issues. While Heath is right to defend against simplistic generalizations on the basis of race, the enormous influence of the history of enslavement in the United States must profoundly influence the performance of black students in mainstream schools.

Oppositional Culture

The influence of racism on education is at the core of another, more satisfying, explanation of our schools' failure to educate African American students: John Ogbu's theory of "oppositional culture," a theory that will lead us to a more comprehensive critique of basic writing. In a series of works over the last decade, Ogbu has attempted to account for the varying degrees of success among many minority groups. If, as Heath, Michaels, and others claim, clashes in cultural style account for minority student failure, Ogbu asks why some groups, with cultural styles that differ widely from the mainstream, don't fail? For example, Ogbu shows that although the Chinese community in Stockton, California, has conversational styles that differ greatly from mainstream styles, their children do not suffer in school performance. Such observations lead Ogbu to conclude that success in school rests on these central contingencies:

> . . . first, whether or not the children come from a segment of society where people have traditionally experienced unequal opportunity to use their literacy skills in a socially and economically meaningful and rewarding manner; and, second, whether or not the relationship between the minorities and the dominant-group members who control the education system has encouraged the minorities to perceive and define acquisition of literacy as an instrument of deculturation without true assimilation. (1974, 151)

Ogbu emphasizes the issues of historically based discrimination and the association of literacy as an instrument of domination. For African American students these issues result in the following skeptical questions about education: "If I learn to do school reading and writing will I compromise my social identity?" and "If I learn to do school reading and writing will I then be economically and socially rewarded?" Note how really different this focus is from both the clash of cultural styles and initiation theory. Instead of wondering how or if African Americans can fit into mainstream school culture, Ogbu's explanation assumes that African American students can fit in, but focuses on the economic, social, and cultural consequences of doing so.

African American students are skeptical of schools' ability to provide them with the means to "get a good job" because they see that it isn't their skills or their education that is the only problem; it's racism. Ogbu argues that because of a history of economic and political oppression, African American cultural identity has developed in opposition to white majority culture; African Americans define themselves, in part, by opposing white culture. And since the white majority dominates schools, to succeed in school is not just irrelevant to economic and social success, it also threatens the social and cultural identity of the successful student.

This oppositional identity, growing from the specific history of slavery, Jim Crow, segregation, and institutional racism, is what differentiates African Americans from other minorities. Success in school means joining the opposition, threatening their identity as black Americans; to do well in school is understood by some as "acting white." Though the strength of this attitude varies from student to student, most African American students feel it to some degree.

The "oppositional culture" explanation of schools' inability to educate African American students explains, in part, why "initiation," let alone "skills," doesn't work as a curricular strategy. The need is not so much to initiate students into the discourse community, to teach them the particular forms of language in the academy. Instead we need to convince students that this community is theirs, that it will not work against their identity and their interests. The following paper illustrates how the conflicting senses of communities shapes writing. It was written by Leon, who was enrolled in the basic writing program at Chico in 1988. In it, Leon demonstrates the effects of "oppositional identity" in both social and psychological terms and in how he structures his discourse. Although the paper is lengthy, I believe that it shows more dramatically than most the degree to which cultural conflicts and continuities can critique and challenge definitions of basic writing. Such a definition calls into question the bases of basic writing programs on two counts, first by virtue of some linguistic or academic deficit, and second by a pedagogy that separates and stratifies.

The boy who saw the light

This pertckler experience in my life started in 1978 and ended in the summer of 1982. This is a story about a boy who finally seen the light before it was to late. This is a story about a boy who was catch between to different world's trying to adjust to them both at the same time not knowing that it would take year's for him to realize that he didn't fit in the one everybody thought he was going to fit in.
This is his experience.

We live in Hawthorne CA, Harwthorne is a quite city it has know gang's volnice if it did it was some crazy white boy punk rock group. When we moved to Hawthorne from Compton it was only about three percent black and latino. That didn't stop me from becoming a member of one the most violent gang's in east L.A. even though I lived miles and miles away from anykind of gang war fare.

The year was 1978 and I was just a young confused little kid at the same time nedding attention if I couldn't get it at home I looked else were. . . .

I have always been one for causing conflict and trying to be different but I didn't know that the stuburnness was going to help get the getto out of my system.

When I went to school with all the white kid's it was a total trip I didn't know how to handle it because 98 percent of the staff and student's were white I couldn't deal.

From a person like me at the time it was a strain on the brain I wasn't use to being the black sheep in the crowd so I conplained to my parent's all the time that the white student's gave me a hard time so I could go to school with my cousin's in the getto. . . .

When I got back to regular classes at school I did better on my work for a while I spoke up more in class and pertisapated in all event's but in all good there's bounded to be some bad somewere in there and it came up.

People were calling me the little rich kid just because I didn't live in the getto know more and even though we weren't rich we were not poor either. That braught me a lot's of problem's I had to prove to them that I was just as wild as they were, back then it was a big then to go to jail luck (uh lee) I never went so I would be tested all the time.

By me living in Hawthorne and going to school in Compton I had to work twice as hard to be tuff at school even though I loved to fight I didn't like beating up people for nothing like many of them did.

Haven't you heard that saying "only the strong will survive" believe me in Compton it's true.

As time progress like most people at my school we all were in a gang it wasn't the same as if someone was asking you to be in there frat, know it was the opposet, either you were down with the gang and help beat people up or not down and get beat up.

It wasn't as bad as it sound's believe me, we played sport's and stuff together it just was some of the stuff I didn't like.

As fight's in the gang arose it affected me in a much more deeper way than just my fist" you see when the day was over I had to get on the bus and go home the rest of them stayed there I didn't. I found it hard for me to deal with both world's, so I went to the stronger of the two. . . .

I came home with a black eye one day my mother didn't say anything but I could tell she was worried but in my cousin's neighborhood people thought that it was just a sign of war scar's preparing you for man hood I gues that's one of the reason's why the name of the gang was nieghborhood ganster C'rip.

As day's passed I found it harder and harder to deal with both world's to me Hawthorne and Compton was two different world's not just two different city's far a part. When I was at home meaning my parent's house I could never set still I was alway's jumppy.

I had white friend's and they use to ask me all the time why do you go to school with those hood's and I would say because I'm a hood, a neighborhood ganster C'rip. When people at my school would ask me if I had white friend's I would say know because they would take it the wrong way, they would take it as a sign of weakness or trying to be white as they say.

This same process went on for a long time intill oneday I meet this old white lady that lived down the street from me she toll me that knew of me and that I wasn't what she exsteced as a gangster. I looked her died in thee eye and smiled then she turned away from me for a minute and then turned right back around and started right back talking. She ended by saying that my face makes people preserve that I'm mean and crazy but just by talking to me and looking into my heart she knew I was a teddy bear. I just laughed and said thank you I have to go . . . .

One morning I woke up extra early so I could talk to my mother. . . . I walked into her room and said (mama) she turned around with a mean look on her face and started to cry I walked toward's her and all of a sudden she slap me in the face my eye's opened up wide because my mother had never hit me before, she didn't scream she just talked and talked for along time I guess that's why it stuck so deep in my head like it did because she never did raise her voice that day.

That night my home boy brandon called me and said everybody is looking for you somebody shot babydee (what) I screamed out over the phone, yo home's brandon said we are going to get throw's fool's back for fucking with our home boy like that.

The next day at school everybody was hyped we all wanted to get them back for shooting baby dee. The fight toke place sometime after school everybody was going to be there I wasn't scared but something inside me toll me that it wasn't right for me anymore even though baby dee was my friend I just didn't want to fight. I was hard to say it even to myself but it was even harder to do. . .

The hour's went by slow every ten minutes I had to use the restroom that was the first time I ever had to shit that much before a gang fight that got me worried because that was a sign of weakness.

Something was wrong I knew it, my brain knew it but my (heart) was it down with my gang no more.

It's an old saying in gang's DO-OR-DIE everybody and every gang lived by that saying it meant that do what you have to do or die like a scared women. It was almost time to go to the fight and what the old white lady and my mother toll me stuck in my head.

It was time to leave to go to the fight and for the first time in my life I wasn't ready, everybody was over my cousin's house ready to walk out the door but I wasn't. I turned to my cousin who was one of the leader's at the time and said lucky, lucky I anit down know more I'm out of here (what he screamed out) he grabed me and said punk you anit shit.

This had been the person that I had admired all this time and he was fronting me in front of everybody when I finally got a grip on everything I hit him and we started fighting he toll all the home boy's what I said and they all started beating me up when they finally got threw beating me up my arm was broke my hand's and mouth were bleeding and my resept was going, in that neighborhood that was you most pride presetion.

I knew that after all of that I could go back to that school anymore so I went back to school were I should have gone in the first place the one right down the street from my house it was hard adjusting but after a while I finally did.

I'm glad that I didn't fight that day because I found out that after the gang fight was over 12 of my home boy's died fighting in that little war. If I would have stayed I could have been one out of those 12 gangsters shot god was looking out for me he most have meant for me to be doing some else besides gang banging.

One thing that Leon's paper demonstrates is the insufficiency of deficit theory or skills approaches in defining basic writing. To see Leon's paper as evidence of "serious multiple skill deficiencies" misrepresents the complexity of his writing. It ignores the complex rhetorical situation that Leon successfully negotiates, that of an urban African American male writing about gangs to a basic writing class in a residential, mostly white university located in a rural area. A skills approach that focuses only on Leon's errors would miss the fact that Leon successfully argues for a particular interpretation of his experience, develops it, and supports it with evidence. A skills approach would focus on minor, easily changed features of Leon's text (such as spelling and punctuation), and suggest to him that his writing is not academic.

I would like to focus on how Ogbu's understanding of literacy can help basic writing teachers understand their students more generously by examining Leon's text in terms of oppositional culture. Although there is something of a genre of "gang papers," this one argues for an explanation; it goes beyond telling a story about the time he almost died. Leon constantly explains his story in the oppositional terms that inform Ogbu's explanation of educational failure. First, let's look at the oppositions themselves. Hawthorne and Compton stand out as the most obvious; they are the "two different worlds." Leon takes pains to show that Hawthorne is white. Note that he doesn't say that Compton is black; black is the unmarked case, the characteristic that is assumed. He writes from this unmarked point of view; he points out the white people.

Neither community allows Leon to move easily from one to the other; these oppositions are socially enforced. We know that Leon feels the tensions because he shows us his discomfort in the white school in Hawthorne. And he shows us why he feels that way: "I had white friends and they use to ask me all the time why do you go to school with those hood's and I would say because I'm a hood, a neighborhood gangster C'rip." But the move outward to Hawthorne makes Compton even more socially dangerous: "People were calling me little rich kid just because I didn't live in the getto know more and even though we weren't rich we weren't poor either." The threat is so great that Leon denies even that he has white friends: "When people at my school would ask me if I had white friend's I would say know because they would take it the wrong way, they would take it as a sign of weakness or trying to be white as they say."

"Weakness" recurs as a threat in Leon's essay and it is associated with whites and with women. Two women figure prominently in shaping Leon's refusal to fight, which he initially characterizes as a weakness. In one sense then, Hawthorne—the location of his mother, the white woman who called him a "teddy bear," and his white friends—is "weakness," and Compton is "strong," the place where "only the strong will survive." The effect of this opposition on Leon's school performance is only suggested in the paragraph that follows his statement that returning to Compton improved his school attitude. He then discusses the pressure to "prove" his belongingness to Compton by working "twice as hard to be tuff at school," and that after refusing to fight he writes that he "could[n't] go back to school anymore." We can infer that success in school in Compton has more to do with toughness, with strength. Success in school in Hawthorne, on the other hand, involves losing respect and strength in Compton.

This strength/weakness opposition is undercut by the end of the essay. The "Do or Die" command is completely reversed; the women, denigrated by him as "scared," have saved his life; the strong have died, and the weak are alive to write.

There is another opposition working in Leon's paper that parallels the Compton/Hawthorne one and is more relevant to how oppositional culture works, and that's the opposition between the university classroom and Compton. This opposition is obvious in phrases like this: "As time progress like most people at my school we all were in a gang it wasn't the same as if someone was asking you to be in there frat, know it was the opposet, either you were down with the gang and help beat people up or not down and get beat up." When Leon writes that "it wasn't the same as if someone was asking you to be in there frat," he's setting up an opposition for the students in the class who were unfamiliar with Compton. He's also aware of the potential ostracism that might occur by disclosing his gang history (he's experienced it already in Hawthorne) and he compensates for that by stating, "It wasn't as bad as it sound's believe me, we played sports and stuff together."

Less obviously there are opposing discourses in Leon's paper that signify this opposition. One strikes me as particularly important: the journalistic exposé that chronicles the escape from the ghetto's gangs and the playful, yet violent discourse of Compton. What makes this paper different from the ordinary gang paper is the continuing presence of the journalistic voice. It is not just present at the beginning and at the end; instead Leon successfully alternates between these discourses. He begins by highlighting *story*, "This is a story," he says twice. The percentages and the sentence, "That didn't stop me from becoming a member of one of the most violent gang's in east L.A.," both present his experiences in the language of an outside observer (such as his teacher and many of his classmates in fraternities). He continues with this perspective when he describes himself as a "confused little kid nedding attention" and when he describes his experience as a "process." This discourse has a counterpoint in Compton, which is playful, sometimes violent, and no less analytical. This is a voice that says, "From a person like me at the time it was a strain on the brain I wasn't use to being the black sheep in the crowd" and, after telling about his black eye, "I guess that's why the name of the gang was the neighborhood ganster C'rip." The Compton discourse, at times, attempts to capture even the phonology of the streets. That's why Leon puts the apostrophe in *C'rip*, so it sounds like how he says it, "Kerrrip." That's also why he spells *luckily: luck (uh lee)*. Sometimes the two discourses coexist in one sentence as in "every ten minutes I had to use the restroom that was the first time I ever had to shit that much before a gang fight." Again, I have to stress that these oppositions are something that Leon himself calls attention to, as in the passage I cited earlier comparing gangs and fraternities.

Although Leon's paper shows us how oppositional cultures work and their effect on education, it isn't itself an example of the negative consequences. "The boy who saw the light" is more an example of successful academic work, where the author articulates cultural oppositions without becoming a victim of them. The essay doesn't pretend to "solve" these conflicts. The competing discourses in Leon's essay reveal competing cultural ideologies. They are certainly not going to be solved by an essay. Just how conscious Leon is about these conflicts is revealed by the following anecdote. Leon's teacher asked him to revise "The boy who saw the light" for an English department publication. In reply, Leon leaned over and said, "You mean 'whiten' it up a little?" Leon's ability to call explicit attention to the cultural and linguistic conflict allows him to participate better in Hawthorne and the university by not having to abandon Compton completely (he retains its language, and he calls upon his experience "there" to help his success "here").

I have called Leon's essay a successful piece of academic work, but I would like to be specific about that claim. First—I don't mean the misspellings (particularly the ones that are not related to Compton speech) or idiosyncratic punctuation. No doubt and no argument, Leon needs to work on his spelling and punctuation. I don't doubt that he can do this with a minimum of effort (this version is a draft). While it is true that Leon does not know how to spell "opposite," he does know how to use literacy to explore and discover the connections and conflicts of two vastly different social scenes. He knows how to use literacy to reflect on and gain wisdom from complex experiences. And he knows how to use literacy to help others share these experiences. These "fundamentals" characterize academic literacy at its best: a focused exploration of a complex topic. Harris argues that writing courses need not "initiate our students into the values and practices of some new community, but to offer them the chance to reflect critically on those discourses—of home, school, work, the media, and the like—to which they already belong" (1989, 19). This seems to be what Leon is up to in "The boy who saw the light," putting together several familiar discourses to try to see where, between Compton and the university, he now wants to live.

As teachers of writing, we need to understand both what is specific about Leon's experience and what generalizations we can make. Ogbu's work shows the importance of understanding the specific history of African Americans and its effects on education. So in some senses, Leon's paper—and what we learn from it—has little to do with, say, the Hmong immigrant who may be in the same class. But Leon's paper can operate as a heuristic device for understanding students whose social and cultural backgrounds conflict with their idea of the university, and that includes many nonnative speakers, Native Americans, Chicanos, Asians, working-class students, gay and lesbian students, and others. The terms of the conflict vary greatly, but the existence of it does not.

Defining student writers as negotiators of cultural conflicts obviously complicates any theory of initiation and makes irrelevant the deficit theory-driven skills and service approaches. The exclusion many students of color feel does not originate in significant differences in discourse forms. It is the result of many factors, among them:

- educational practices that create the belief that large gaps exist between what students know and what students need to know, which stem from mistaken ideas about the value and characteristics of both students' discourse and academic discourse;
- racism, classism, and sexism, conscious or unconscious beliefs that working-class students, students of color, and women students really do not belong in the university because they are different; and
- institutional histories that produce standards based on reduced ideas of literacy.

Given these reasons, the ground beneath basic writing—as a concept and as a program—starts to shake. Although many students, and many students of color, find support and strength in writing courses, we need to find institutional structures that do not further marginalize students of color and that do not underestimate their literacy. We are obligated to help our students gain access to the university so that by virtue of their participation they redefine it more democratically.

David Bartholomae's recent article, "The Tidy House: Basic Writing and the American Curriculum," explores the way that basic writing works as an institutional projection of liberalism. Bartholomae's work shows us how basic writing has reproduced an unsatisfactory accommodation of "access" and "gatekeeping":

> The Basic Writing program, then, can be seen simultaneously as an attempt to bridge AND preserve cultural difference, to enable students to enter the "normal" curriculum but to insure, at the same time, that there are basic writers. (1993, 9)

Bartholomae's argument is important because he discloses the way that our standards of discrimination between "basic" and "normal" rest on assumptions about texts. These assumptions would deny a text like Leon's a generous reading, or a reading that would allow Leon academic power. Bartholomae has long critiqued the domination of simplistically unified texts. In "The Tidy House" this criticism takes on a sharper edge, showing how the "topic sentence, the controlling idea, gathering together of ideas that fit while excluding, outlawing those that don't (the overwhelming, compelling specifics)" (1993, 15) work together with the discourse of liberalism that justifies distinctions between basic and normal writers: "basic writers are produced by our desires to be liberals—to enforce a commonness among our students by making the differences superficial, surface-level, and by designing a curriculum to both insure them and erase them in 14 weeks" (1993, 12).

Given these critiques of the institutional structure and ideologies of writing courses, the task of taking responsibility for the limited participation by students of color in higher education is not a clear or easy one. It is clear that at the very least, we need to eliminate basic writing structures that delay entrance into the academy. In addition to political action both in and outside the university against racism, we need to get our own house in order. Without denying the need for many students to receive additional support and time with their writing, we need to work to ameliorate the punitive and gatekeeping functions of writing courses. Certainly that means exploring institutional changes, but it also means constantly critiquing ideologies that reduce writing courses to service and skills.

Writing teachers, themselves underestimated by university structures, understand from the inside how schools unequally distribute authority. By claiming the expertise over literacy, writing teachers and administrators can enter into the ideological definition of "standards" in order to argue that students like Leon belong in the university. To do so, the work demanded of them goes beyond their work in the classroom. They must also, despite their lack of institutional authority, enter into the mire of institutional change, and transform those structures that work against access.

Chapter Four

Standards and Political Change

This chapter moves from the examination of historical circumstances of standards and access to an exploration of how writing program administrators can work within universities to increase access. While the focus of the chapter is on actual practices at my university, the programs represented by the three cases are typical: basic and first-year composition, writing across the curriculum, and a university-school program (in this case, a National Writing Project site). By examining these cases together I am making the argument for a coordinated practice—one that recognizes that the difficulty of increasing access involves work simultaneously across multiple programs and sites.

Standards in a Local Context

We normally say that we "have" or "hold" standards, but standards, especially because of their political nature, are always an action. Historically and currently standards conserve and retain; their use is central to those who wish nostalgically for a monocultural university. Consider the following two examples from my campus, vastly different in approach and tone, yet each using standards as a way of social sorting.

At the beginning of the school year in 1990, deans of the university, the University Writing Committee, and department chairs were surprised to receive a memo about writing from the provost. Its subject was underlined twice: "All-Campus Responsibility for Writing:

71

Departmental Standards." The first paragraph begins by historically situating writing instruction at CSU, Chico:

> Thanks to the hard work of dedicated faculty throughout the campus, the level of student writing at Chico has significantly improved over the past decade. As departments developed and refined writing proficiency programs, students and faculty have increasingly become aware that writing is central to the learning process. It now seems a good time to reevaluate where we stand on the all-campus responsibility for student writing and to take the next evolutionary step—the installation of writing effectiveness approaches in all courses throughout the major.

That's a remarkable first sentence. At the very least, our ex-provost (he has since resigned) did not fall into the trap of the hysterical and repeated proclamation of declining literacy. I imagine that many writing faculty would be delighted to have a provost recognize their program in this way; imagine, "students and faculty have increasingly become aware that writing is central to the learning process." Of course, there are bits to complain about; "learning process" usually suggests a cognitive model of knowledge acquisition, but that's a trifle.

The next sentence is straighforwardly disingenuous, an example of what Thia Wolf cites as "schizophrenic" language, typical of institutions: While the provost states that it's a "good time to reevaluate where we (faculty?) stand," this reevaluation seems to have already occurred; not only that, but the next step—an action, signaled by a bold-faced "Action Required" opposite the provost's signature, has already been decided upon, too. That next step, which is not *revolutionary*, but only "evolutionary," is "the installation of writing effectiveness approaches in all courses throughout the major." *Installation* is an unusual word to use for a pedagogy. And "writing effectiveness approaches" is a term that lacks a credible opposite.

The third paragraph deals more directly with departmental standards:

> [Writing Proficiency] courses need reinforcement from the entire department to assure that the writing standards expected in a WP course are also expected everywhere student writing is required in the major. This goal can be achieved only if faculty expect student writing to meet demanding department standards, if they accept only work that does, and if they define writing standards that are appropriate for their specific disciplines—standards determined in part by the kinds of writing students will need to compete successfully in graduate school or in their chosen fields.

I am aware that composition faculty on many campuses would be delighted to have a provost who is both enlightened about the nature of discipline-specific writing and who is so committed to writing. The memo focuses on disciplinary standards and also acknowledges that these standards are plural, varying from discipline to discipline. Later in the memo, he even states that the standards within each department may vary and need to take "into account . . . the various conditions and purposes of academic writing both formal and informal." He does tie together easily writing achievement and success, stating that the standards for each department are "determined in part by the kinds of writing students will need to compete successfully in graduate school or in their chosen fields."

Still, there's a nagging conflict between the plurality of writing in disciplines and a focus on standards that seems completely unnecessary. If the provost wished to have "writing effectiveness approaches" installed (by composition installers?) in all courses, then that aim does not necessarily have to result in a department having to determine standards for their "Strategic Plan Update." Standards seem decidedly out of place; after all, student writing has "significantly improved." Part of the memorandum seems like a pleasant invitation to incorporate discipline-specific writing in all courses in the major. Another part is a demand to administrators to tighten writing standards in all courses in the major, not just the WP course. The actual demand doesn't come until the last sentence: "Please attach copies of the newly developed standards to your 1991–1992 Strategic Plan Update."

What is significant about this memo is that despite its progressive and informed nature and its assuredness about the course of action, given the practical politics of everyday life on our campus, it did not further the goals of writing faculty on our campus, it actually hindered them. The memo uses what Burke would call a rhetoric of identification; it identifies required writing standards as an administrative goal with what had been, until this memo, a faculty-driven, faculty-based Writing Across the Disciplines program. The faculty movement was praised, but by the end of the memo that movement was appropriated by the provost's office and "the next step" that seemingly came from the faculty movement was commanded by the administration. Notably absent in the memo is the provost's reasoning: the purpose behind the memo. His only stated goal is that WP courses need "reinforcement."

My goal in this discussion is not to claim that our provost was being especially devious, but to demonstrate that power in the university works in complicated and opaque ways. Standards are a major means of exercising power. While this memo is—on the surface—surprisingly supportive of decentralized standards, its effect on our campus was to damage more substantive ideological work done by the University Writing Committee and the Writing Across the Disciplines program.

Domination, if one can even attach that word to the above memo, does not always occur so subtly, even in the political labyrinth of the university. The following letter to the editor in our local daily paper, *The Enterprise-Record,* is more blatant in its association of access with falling standards:

> In your Feb. 20 article on the American Indian symposium at CSUC, Indian student leader Eddie Webb is quoted as saying, "Why can't we have a Native American teaching Native American studies and literature?"
>
> As a member of the History Department of CSUC, I can answer his question so far as the teaching of Indian history is concerned.
>
> For the history department, for all practical purposes, qualified faculty of Indian extraction do not exist. The American Historical Association informs us that, in 1992, the nation's universities did not grant a Ph.D. in history—any kind of history—to a single Native American! This despite a decade of strenuous recruitment by the profession.
>
> What about Indians who already have Ph.D's? Because of Affirmative Action, historians of Indian extraction, like women, black, Chicanos, and other protected classes, get jobs at higher salaries and at far more prestigious universities than they could have dreamed of winning had they been white males.
>
> That is, and speaking generally, of course, the Indians, etc., at Harvard would never have been considered for elevation to the crimson had they not been Indians. The Indians, etc., at state-supported research universities, would be at teaching institutions of the CSUC type were they not Indians. By the time you get to the level of CSUC— speaking generally again—little more is required of Affirmative Action faculty than that they show evidence of a majority of vital life signs.
>
> CSUC's principal historian of American Indians has demonstrated an intelligence, sensitivity to Indian students, and teaching ability that would have her in the Ivy League, or very close to it, if she were not Caucasian. . . .
>
> [Native Americans] are at CSUC to get the best possible education, including education in the past ways and woes of the people from whom they are genetically descended. They are not here to have their sensibilities stroked and grades of A doled out on the basis of their race or correct politics. (Conlin 1993)

This letter represents a view of access and standards that has evolved over the last century and a half in the United States. Its assumptions are fairly mainstream, that standards are supposed to conserve, and that members of the academy who didn't used to be there (Native Americans in this case) lower standards by their presence. The remarkable hierarchy of institutions—from the elevated crimson (where apparently everyone wants to work) to the "level of the CSUC," a teaching institution—plays a dual role. First, it is aimed at faculty of color, who only have to "show evidence of a majority of vital signs" to receive tenure. Secondly, it serves to belittle the whole institution. The cause? Unqualified people of color. The standards and access binary are not only applied to faculty, but by the last sentence of the letter, also applied to students of color who seem to be asking not "Why can't we have a Native American teaching Native American studies and literature?" but to have their sensibilities stroked and be given A grades.

This letter did not emerge from a single individual with isolated opinions. The many supportive responses to this letter made this clear, frequently citing the "common sense" of the letter, implying that all the author did was tell the truth. The "commonsense" argument response signals hegemony at work. Undefined or vague standards (usually simply resting on status quo conditions) remain a primary tool of hegemony against access. There was also articulate protest from Native Americans, among them Eddie Webb, and also from many faculty.

Deeply entrenched in the university, and in education in general, are the series of assumptions and practices that work against access. These two examples show how indirect and direct these assumptions and practices can be. The university's power to exclude is often neither direct nor centralized. As a meritocracy, it operates on ideologies of individualism and competition. And backing it up are seemingly ahistorical standards that putatively distinguish between the smart and the stupid, the hard-working and the lazy. The means for measuring students against these standards are also putatively neutral, tests and paper topics where "everyone" gets treated fairly. And yet, the results—again, not only from these contexts—are that people of color often feel neither welcome nor capable in educational institutions.

The question of how to work against the gatekeeping functions of the university is a very difficult one. The letter above shows how pervasive the ideology is that pits access against standards. Additionally, actual structures of the university also support this ideology: no-credit basic writing, the series of placement and proficiency tests that exist on most campuses, the first-year composition requirement for all students, and bureaucratic inertia that so slows down the process of change that activists retire before the process is finished. Political action that would change the reproductive function of the university would not be simple reform, it would be a reversal. It is foolish to underestimate this opposition or imagine that anything but sustained, determined work is going to change higher education so that it works in the interests of people of color.

In this chapter I'll describe a set of interconnected administrative practices by the composition faculty as political activity. My claim is that these practices are political. They are acts of resistance to ideologies and actions in the university that oppose access, ideologies and actions that, as should be unsurprising by now, frequently come in the form of arguments about standards. These administrative practices are neither random or uncoordinated, nor could they be planned and predictable. Yet I can describe them as political in a fairly precise way: (1) they seek to dislodge ideologies, educational structures, and teaching practices that reproduce existing social hierarchies; (2) they build social networks or coalitions that extend communication across class boundaries (both as defined in purely educational ways such as "student" and "teacher," and defined in more traditional ways), and disciplinary boundaries; (3) they seek coalitions with coworkers at other levels of institutions; and (4) they resist, forestall, or foil institutional actions that would further restrict access.

The political activity I seek to describe is not, on the whole, what would normally be called "revolutionary," at least not in the sense that it will lead quickly to a permanent disruption of the status quo. By necessity it works in locations and structures defined by the institution. Because it is ideological work, work that critiques dominant ideas of literacy and argues for new ones, its location is everywhere and anywhere. Because it is also practical activity it involves teaching, policy making, administration, committee work, and lobbying.

This kind of political activity acknowledges that no sudden overthrow of the state is imminent, and that revolutionary practice in the traditional marxist conception is, at this point in history, delusional. Currently, the most generative model for political activity that acknowledges the sense of dominance that can at once appear as directly as in the anti-affirmative action letter or as indirectly as in the provost's memo is Antonio Gramsci's "war of position." Evan Watkins' description of the term in *Work Time* is helpful, noting that Gramsci proposed a mode of revolutionary activity that was appropriate to the way that power operated in Western economies and was opposed to Russian models:

> . . . the historical development of capitalism in at least certain European nations and the United States results in the initially stupefying illusion that power is simultaneously everywhere and nowhere; no sooner is one "fortress" demolished than still another one appears. The "war" then necessarily becomes a war *of position* rather than an encircling maneuver. (1971, 50)

In what may be either a preparatory move or a prolonged way of working, the war of position contrasts with a sudden overthrow of the state. The war of position is siege warfare against hegemony and "requires exceptional qualities of patience and inventiveness" (Gramsci 1971, 239). While the war of position may seem like an abandonment of revolutionary activity (as some have argued), Watkins makes the case that the war of position is not just the only conception of action available, but also the political strategy that best takes advantage of the weakness in the seemingly all-powerful hegemony:

> The very expansiveness of the modern and bourgeois-dominated State, its involvement in some way in every facet of social life, on the one hand makes an ultimately decisive war of maneuver impossible, but at the same time it marks a limit to State power. For as a complex ensemble of relations rather than a homogeneous instrument of domination, it is vulnerable to pressure at countless points. (Gramsci 1971, 52)

The very widespread nature of the hegemony that insists that standards and access are opposed, then, is exactly what makes a war of position not only possible, but appropriate. The fact that it operates in so many contexts and levels, rather than from a centralized source, makes small change at many locations possible.

This idea of political action heightens the role that language and rhetoric play in change. As Victor Villaneuva makes clear in *Bootstraps*, a war of position, like hegemony itself, is waged through language. As activists persuade, argue, and challenge, they win agreement. In so doing they form a collective, a new "counter" hegemony, what Gramsci calls a new "historic bloc" that can bring about a new hegemony (Villaneuva 1993, 126). Central to the whole process is "active rhetorical practice" (Villaneuva 1993, 126).

Watkins and Villaneuva's descriptions of a war of position within English departments help make Gramsci's rather sketchy concept more useful. And yet, even with the useful discussions of the war of position in regards to English departments, this concept is not much elaborated. To these unelaborated descriptions, I would like to add one more, Raymond Williams' helpful description of the "long revolution":

> The nature of the process indicates a perhaps unusual revolutionary activity: open discussion, extending relationship, the practical shaping of institutions. But it indicates also a necessary strength: against arbitrary power whether of arms or of money, against all conscious confusion and weakening of the long and difficult human effort, and for and with the people who in many different ways are keeping the revolution going. (1961, 355)

Williams' formulation, which like Gramsci's, came under fire for being too "gradualist," but it seems to me to provide a way of working in universities and colleges that is neither deluded nor cynical: open discussion, extending relationships, the practical shaping of institutions.

Neither Gramsci nor Williams offer, nor do many of their commentators in English offer, much in the way of specific actions that would constitute a "war of position." Villaneuva discusses curricular changes in the basic writing program as an example of counterhegemonic action

("On Writing Groups"), and Watkins argues somewhat abstractly that "English" should act as a "support structure" for popular practices that resist hegemony (1989, 264). Yet the concrete description of what constitutes effective political practice remains fairly unelaborated, partly because of the difficulty of discerning what counts as effective.

Writing-program administrators and instructors, as shown in the various contexts that I have explored in the last two chapters, have influence over many of the points of access between the university and currently excluded social groups. Part of the power of composition programs, which is simultaneously their vulnerability, is their service nature—the assumption by the university that first-year composition will teach general skills, skills that will prepare students and, therefore, provide access to various specialized disciplines. Both for students (see Anderson et al. 1990) and for composition faculty, this idea of preparation seems theoretically bankrupt as well as pragmatically impossible. How could we prepare students—in one semester—for the fundamentals of writing in engineering, nursing, history, business, and chemistry? The impossibility of that task simply reminds us that we are valued for another purpose, what Watkins calls the "intraeducational dilemma of sorting out student abilities" (1989, 108). The generality of the standards marks this. Yet the widespread institutionalization of composition, and the growing trend to hire full-time, tenure-track faculty educated in composition studies to administer writing tests and teach in writing programs gives composition administrators and teachers (and also students) a series of opportunities to transform the gatekeeping functions of these institutional sites.

Writing Programs and Political Action at CSU, Chico

Since my argument about standards depends on seeing standards working at specific locations, it makes sense to argue for the value of the local when discussing political action. I have two aims: The first is to describe real events that I see as working to increase access and in so doing ground the notions of political action in real actions. The second is to extend the notions of political action discussed by Gramsci, Williams, and their commentators.

In this discussion, I will be referring to three parts of CSU, Chico's writing program during the mid-1990s: the basic/first-year composition program, coordinated by Judith Rodby; the Writing Across the Disciplines program co-coordinated by Thia Wolf, Elizabeth Renfro, and Lauren Wright; and the Northern California Writing Project, which I direct. Because I want to be specific about political action, I will be concentrating on three fairly discrete events: the elimination of the basic writing program, the response to the Provost's standards memo by the Writing Across the Disciplines program, and a publication project sponsored by the Northern California Writing Project. Readers should know that these programs have changed dramatically since my research, particularly the Writing Across the Disciplines program, which was cut dramatically in the late 1980s. Thia Wolf no longer directs that program.

I would like to emphasize several features of this political activity that seem to distinguish my discussion somewhat from other commentators. First, and probably most important, is that this political activity was both coordinated and collaborative. That is, the three tenured composition faculty, Tom Fox, Judith Rodby, and Thia Wolf, believed that work done in institutionally discrete parts of the composition program can contribute to similar educational goals, one of which is increased access for people of color, women, and working-class students. Occasionally, we have explicitly discussed this collaboration, and we worked out procedures for information and decision sharing. At other times, the sense of collaboration was more tacit. And there are still other times when it seemed absent. While the tactics and strategies used to achieve the general goal of increased access varied widely (even in a single program), most often there was a sense that, as program coordinators, we were in this together, and that the actions our programs took separately became more meaningful because they were coordinated, perhaps loosely, with actions taken in other programs.

This was possible because of the strange combination of power and powerlessness that characterizes writing program administrators in modern universities. Michel de Certeau in *The Practice of Everyday Life* describes two kinds of political action: "strategies," which are the domain of the powerful, and "tactics," which are "an art of the weak" (1984, 37). As a writing program administrator, I find myself blending the two. Strategies, according to de Certeau, are long-term and general. They depend on "place," defined broadly by de Certeau. Place could mean anything from "a research laboratory" to perhaps something like a "writing program." Strategies, because they emerge from a power base, appear to have more autonomy than tactics. By contrast, tactics occur on the space of the powerful. Tactics are best illustrated by de Certeau's example of *la perruque*, the practice of workers engaging in noninstitutional activities (writing letters, reading for pleasure, borrowing tools) on company time. De Certeau argues that "tactics" depend on time more than place, because their action is a diversion of time from the employer. Tactics are a "last resort," they cannot be coordinated because they depend on the opportunity provided by the institution. Practitioners of tactics must be watchful, and "accept the chance offerings of the moment, and seize on the wing the possibilities that offer themselves"

(1984, 37). The events described below fall somewhere between strategies and tactics. Clearly, all of our writing programs were operating in institutional sites that were primarily defined by others, so it would follow that all our actions were tactical. Yet there was a regularity to the kinds of tactics we employed that defined our actions as something more strategic than what de Certeau describes.

With this framework of political activity, I would like to enter into a more elaborated—and by necessity more institutionally specific— discussion of the work of composition professors in English departments in order to illustrate the practical political activity that can reconceive the institutionalized relationship between standards and access.

Standards, Access, Economics, and Eliminating Basic Writing

In Chapter 3, I referred to the state of California's Master Plan, last renewed in 1987, which sets the policy for remedial education in the three levels of higher education in California, noting that it defines basic writers in deficit terms. This definition justified the policy that basic writing courses could not receive baccalaureate credit. It represents a policy clearly in the tradition of gatekeeping. The punish in this system of discipline is that the funding used to support these classes is tied to the official definition of "remedial" as no-credit. Judith Rodby describes this circular logic in her article, "What It's For and What It's Worth?":

> . . . the no-credit arrangement was continually naturalized through a series of circular moves: We were told that remedial courses cannot receive credit because they are remedial and the university does not give credit for remedial courses; we were also told that our campus cannot give credit for [basic writing] courses because we only offer one semester of freshman writing for credit, and so those courses must be classified as remedial. (1996, 108)

If our campus were to try to offer baccalaureate credit for these courses, then we would lose funding for the courses. CSU, Chico, had tried a number of initiatives to change this policy; none met with any success.

There were, of course, many complaints from the students. In part because of a pedagogy that invited dialogue, many students felt free to critique the course. One semester several students wrote letters to leaders in public education in California, describing their sense of oppression. Teachers, too, became frustrated with the no-credit course, and while sympathizing with their students' opinions, nonetheless found it a difficult course to teach. When I turned over the coordination of the program to my colleague Judith Rodby in 1990, the program had settled into an uncomfortable stasis.

During the first two years of her stint as basic writing coordinator, Rodby interviewed faculty and students. She became more and more convinced that the oppressive structure of the program limited teachers' abilities and disabled their classrooms, overshadowing the best teaching or the most relevant curriculum:

> . . . it did not matter whether we thought of and called the program remedial, basic, or developmental writing. It did not finally matter how relevant, insightful, or provocative our curriculum was. No remedial courses in the California State University carried credit, and our students were finally not able to accept the worth of courses that gave them no credit. (Rodby 1996, 108)

In a series of meetings and conversations, Rodby began to demonstrate to faculty, often indirectly, that the concept of basic writing rested upon a notion that the skills learned in the conditions of the basic writing class "transferred" to first-year composition, a notion that she argued, given the institutional separation of credit and no-credit, was false. She argued against the notion of general and transferable skills that Watkins and Miller cite as a central means by which English functions as social sorter.

In 1992, the budget situation was so bad that each campus received a memo from the chancellor's office stating that the money distributed to each campus for the purpose of remedial writing would "no longer be monitored."

Ironically, then, the budget crisis produced an opportunity to free the constraints of the basic writing program organization. After a great deal of thinking, discussing, and conducting research, Rodby made the decision to eliminate basic writing, both as a program and as a concept:

> Conceptually, we abandoned the terms basic writing and remediation as we began to see that they were primarily institutional "slots," interchangeable terms for what the institution saw as one monolithic problem. (Rodby 1996, 108)

She proposed a new model of first-year composition that would mainstream basic writers but retain extra support for those students who needed it. Having already done a great deal of rhetorical work, Rodby secured the support for the proposal from the English Department Curriculum Committee, and the strong and informed support of the chair, Carol Burr. It seemed like a done deal.

It is no accident, however, that the actual money for the basic writing program is not distributed by the English Department. Given the definition of writing—and especially basic writing—as a generalized skill, the basic writing program, at the level of distribution of funds, was administered by the provost's office. All of us involved in the proposal underestimated the effect this would have. When the assistant to the vice president for academic affairs received the proposal, she balked, stating, "Shared programs demand shared decisions."

Williams, Watkins, and Gramsci all stress that the political work of a "war of position" demands, among other things, patience. Despite her outrage over the administration's interference in departmental curriculum, Rodby had no choice but to accept that decision. To regain a sense of progress (and to establish a sense of inevitable change), she proposed a pilot program to show the possibilities of her idea, and eventually persuaded the assistant to the vice president for academic affairs to accept the change.

In this war of position, Rodby fought both structural constraints: systems of funding, hierarchies of authority, state mandates. She also fought ideologies of knowledge: assumptions about standards, contexts, and literacy. Both the structures and the ideologies worked against access; the changes, we hoped, would remove some of the institutional barriers facing those students who used to be in basic writing. This work is exhausting because it demands relentless pressure and patience in all kinds of situations, from formal presentations at curriculum committees to informal discussions while walking to the parking lots. Considering the obstacles to this change, Rodby's success was remarkable.

No one should underestimate Rodby's efforts in changing the structure of writing in first-year programs, nor should we pretend that changing that alone constitutes political change of great significance. For the changes in first-year composition to be politically effective—even on the small, internal level of our writing program—many other changes needed to accompany it. Obviously, the remedial history of first-year composition remains, and either we need to eliminate that course, or transform the ideologies surrounding it, which would not only involve the rest of the university, but also the expectations of students as they enter. Additionally changes in first-year writing need to be supported by the writing contexts that follow it.

Writing Across the Disciplines

Many specialists in composition administer or have access to Writing Across the Curriculum programs. While constantly threatened by funding issues, these programs nonetheless provide an important occasion for faculty to get together to explore, critique, and extend their teaching. Although not unique in this characteristic, Chico's Writing Across the Disciplines (WAD) program has had the benefit of a long history, a history that is distinguished in that it has been primarily "owned" by faculty. It existed without much institutional support for many years and was identified by faculty as a *faculty* program (see Fulwiler and Young for a description of the program as it existed in 1988). The program was run by a variety of people in a variety of roles; in 1989, Thia Wolf was hired to join the program as the first tenure-track hire. From 1989 to 1994, WAD was co-coordinated by Elizabeth Renfro (who had participated in and administered WAD nearly since its inception), Wolf, and an additional coordinator from another discipline. As the program evolved in the early 1990s, it began to explore politically charged issues of race, class, and gender.

It is in the context of the beginning of this evolution that I would like to recount a chronology of events that demonstrates WAD's participation in the rhetorical reshaping of the standards/access binary. These events do not, in most instances, represent cause and effect. Instead, they demonstrate the pervasive ideology of standards as conserving, and the repeated attempts by the program to represent standards differently. First, for reference, here is a chronology of events, without comment:

1. April 1990. Diversity conference proposed by Elizabeth Renfro and Tom Fox. Funding denied by a faculty committee.

2. August 1990. Provost's standards memo, with attachment by the assistant to the vice president for academic affairs.

3. October 1990. Thia Wolf's response to the standards memo from the University Writing Committee.

4. November 1990. Diversity and Classroom Practice workshop announced in the WAD newsletter.

5. January 1991. Diversity and Classroom Practice workshop took place; discussion of standards by faculty occurs.

6. March 1991. "Thoughts on Writing 'Standards'" reports of the faculty discussion in the lead article in the WAD newsletter.

The first item on the chronology is a campuswide conference on diversity that Renfro and I proposed, the central purpose of which was to "introduce faculty to the ways that gender, class, and race affect student writing and learning." When we proposed this conference in memo form, we used our positions as administrators to signal that this conference was a joint proposal of two programs, WAD (Renfro) and the basic writing program (which at that time I coordinated). This proposal was denied funding by the Faculty Recognition and Support Committee.

About this same time, the faculty grassroots image of WAD was administratively challenged in two ways. The first was the provost's proposal that all new faculty be *required* to participate in an introductory

WAD workshop, a proposal reluctantly accepted by the program (a move that Wolf now characterizes as an error). The second challenge came in August of 1990, when the provost's standards memo was issued. Although the memo itself does not mention WAD, it came with an attachment from the assistant to the vice president for academic affairs, stating that "WAD workshops will be available to faculty requesting help in developing departmental standards in writing." The attachment also gave examples of the "type of inquiry" that might be made in the document that was to issue from the standards requirement. One of the examples was to identify faculty who had been involved in WAD.

I want to reiterate that one way to look at these moves by the provost's office was to see them as institutional support of the work of the Writing Across the Disciplines program; certainly that was the official view and the sincere view of some members of the provost's office. However, the salient point is that the language of the memo, plus the additional bureaucratic requirement, raised the concern among WAD coordinators that faculty would resist the standards initiative and identify WAD with an imposing central administration.

Thia Wolf and Elizabeth Renfro felt it was crucial that if WAD was to continue to be faculty-based, then it would have to distinguish itself from the administration's effort with standards. In a move that de Certeau would characterize as a "tactic," Wolf, who was also chair of the University Writing Committee (UWC), wrote a memo summarizing the discussion of the UWC and had it distributed to chairs. In that memo she recast the standards memo in substantive ways. First, she changed the location of the faculty alliance. Both the provost's memo and the attachment suggested that WAD would act as a consulting body. The memo from Wolf clearly suggested that the UWC—a more bureaucratic entity—would be the consulting body: "The University Writing Committee is willing to act as a consulting body to departments across the campus in this matter and as an advisory body to the Provost's Office." The syntax even suggests that the UWC *was asked* by the provost's office to do this. Nowhere in the memo is WAD mentioned. Additionally, Wolf recast the whole task of writing standards, suggesting to faculty, chairs, and deans ways for the standards requirement to become something other than a new set of rules to exclude students.

> During [the UWC's] meeting, we agreed that the purpose of the writing standards requirement was three-fold:
> a. to promote conversation within departments about the kinds of writing professors actually require and the criteria by which such writing is evaluated.
> b. to develop a written description of the kinds of writing assigned within departments. This description would serve as an aid to new faculty who are asked to include writing in their courses and as a

reminder to all faculty about the kinds of writing deemed appropriate and useful within a discipline.

c. to encourage individual faculty to provide their students with written descriptions of writing assignments and evaluative criteria on a course-by-course basis.

In this memo, Wolf shifted the provost's emphasis on defining written standards to a more open and plural view: a conversation about the kinds of writing professors assign and the ways that they evaluate it. Wolf's memo effectively shifted the provost's requirement for an uncritical and prescriptive definition of standards to a descriptive request (which, if discussed, holds possibility for critical reflection).

Wolf's memo demonstrates the important ways that tactics work as a rhetorical response to domination. Although the institutional ground—de Certeau's space—was clearly the central administration's, because of the diversity of bureaucratic hegemony, Wolf found cracks by using the University Writing Committee as a buffer for the potentially more radical WAD program.

WAD, however, was not finished with the standards issue, and this time took a more strategic tack. Strategies, de Certeau reminds us, depend on a mastery of space. Although WAD's existence depended on funding from administrative sources, WAD had two "spaces" from which to launch strategic moves. The first was the faculty workshop and the second was a well-respected newsletter edited by Renfro called *Literacy and Learning*, which was distributed to all faculty. It was highly thought of by the faculty.

In November of 1990, *Literacy and Learning*'s front page was a collage of quotations; the top four quotations, two from students (a Native American and a woman) and two from published authors of color, all argued for language standards that would enable access, standards that would be more plural. The bottom three quotations were all from professors, and all reiterated the traditional view of standards, including an S. I. Hayakawa statement on English-Only. In the middle of these quotations was the announcement for the WAD workshop on "Diversity and Classroom Practice," the aim of which was to "explore the ways in which race, class, and gender diversity in our classrooms offer challenges and opportunities for both teachers and students." The workshop was held to a full crowd in January of 1991 and, in March, newsletter editor Renfro used the workshop occasion to confront the standards memo. The article begins with Raymond Williams' gloss on standards from *Keywords*, cited earlier in this book. Williams' quotation historicizes standards and criticizes their use as "a generalized version of the essence of civilization" (1983, 298). Renfro follows this quotation with a report on a faculty discussion of standards that occurred during the diversity workshop. The agent of nearly every assertion in Renfro's memo is "faculty," which besides being true to the discussion at the workshop, also realigns WAD with its traditional base among faculty. This strategy also allows WAD to challenge more directly the assumptions about standards in the provost's memo while speaking in another voice. For instance, the second paragraph undercuts the notion of standards present in the provost's memo as pedagogically unwise and pragmatically impossible:

> Faculty uniformly agreed that uniform agreement among their colleagues about what constitutes "good writing"—even if restricted to just one particular department—is virtually impossible. And many questioned its desirability, seeing prescriptive "standards of acceptability" as antithetical to instructor's individual approaches and emphases in teaching.

The article ends with questions that the faculty brainstormed, many of which deal directly with standards and their relationship with access, especially the last two:

> What about "writing with an accent" and the application of standards? (In California, one in six elementary school students does not speak English at home)

> How are we using these standards? As a screen for "incompetents" or as teaching tools to empower our students to be successful?

Departments, of course, still had to respond to the provost's memo, and many, I imagine, did so bureaucratically. Several departments, however, with the encouragement of the UWC, actually had a conversation about standards and their use. In so doing, they resisted the gatekeeping request of the standards memo, and used the occasion to reflect on, and perhaps change, their understanding of standards.

Extending Relationships: A Publication Project with an NWP Site

The National Writing Project, with its 157 sites across the country, has been transforming literacy instruction for nearly twenty years. Its central feature is a Summer Institute for public school teachers where a main feature of the curriculum is teachers' inquiry into successful practices in the teaching of writing. These institutes are invitational: Successful teachers teach other successful teachers. Almost all institutes are connected with a university or college and are usually held on university campuses. There are two leaders for each institute; one is from the university and one is a K–12 teacher. Since the mid 1980s, all sites in California explicitly seek to improve the education of disenfranchised students.

This model, developed by James Gray in 1974, challenges usual university activity toward K–12 schooling and challenges usual staff development for teachers. The usual university practice in preservice education wields research as expertise against teacher experience and knowledge. The usual teacher inservice brings in an outside expert, who often has little teaching experience, to lecture or lead activities for a group of teachers working in a context that the expert has little knowledge about. The NWP's Summer Institutes bring together teacher leaders in the field of writing from all grade levels and subjects to share and critique their own practices, current research, and their own professional and personal writing.

While this model is not intrinsically radical, it certainly sets up conversations that are unlikely to occur in other educational contexts. University professors still have expertise, but it is appropriately limited and does not extend beyond the context in which he or she works, and does not dominate the expertise of the teachers. CSU, Chico has one of the oldest NWP sites, started in 1976 by a foresighted Louise Jensen, a professor of linguistics in the English department. After meeting with Gray, Jensen began the Northern California Writing Project, modeled after Gray's Bay Area Writing Project, and saw it through several years of scarce funding. In 1988, she invited me to collaborate with her in leading the project, eventually I assumed the full directorship in 1994. It is within this context, a well-established site that challenges traditional educational hierarchies, that I narrate the story of a student publication sponsored by the statewide California Writing Project.

The project began with a teacher, Jo Walser, who attended the Summer Institute in 1989 and an advanced workshop on teacher-research in 1990. In the teacher-research workshop we read several ethnographies, among them Heath's *Ways with Words* and selections from John Ogbu's work. Walser was keenly interested in these selections and talked to the group about Elk Creek alternative school, which was her current teaching assignment.

Elk Creek is located in a remote valley on the eastern slope of the Coast Range in central California. About five miles from the small town of Elk Creek is a small rancheria, "Grindstone," home to about 120 Native Americans. Grindstone is distinguished by what is said to be the largest roundhouse in California, in which seasonal dances—The Great Big Head dance and other dances—occur. The children from Grindstone attend the main school at Elk Creek where they are a small but significant minority. It will not surprise anyone familiar with schooling to know that the school typically failed the children of the Grindstone. Most children from Grindstone did not graduate, and the teachers couldn't remember the last time the school graduated a female Native American.

In part the blame is on history—the destruction and abuse of Native Americans in California as elsewhere. Elk Creek is full of the specifics of this historical abuse: the mine where stolen Indian children were stowed, the many sites of battles with whites. Schools have been part of the colonizing of California, and it is little wonder that they are not meant to serve the interests of Native Americans. Walser recognized this, and also that choices for change were limited.

Knowing that the California Writing Project was committed to improving the education of students of color, I approached Walser and asked if she thought the writing project could do anything at the school. Walser went back to her school, and—as is typical of her style—spoke with the janitor, who was one of the few Indians working at the school. Walser and the janitor came up with a publication project, a student-written collection of essays and stories that would represent both the Indian community and the white community. The collection would primarily be written by the students of the alternative school, but the rest of the school could contribute, too.

It took three years to complete the project. During the first two years, Walser worked to show skeptical alternative school students the value of the project. While the project had grass roots in that the janitor was part of the source of the idea, students at first rightly saw it as the teacher's project. Walser, however, is an unusual teacher, unusually straightforward, unusually committed. Sometime during the first six months, the students began to see the "book" as theirs. Indian students contributed many pieces that brought to the public eye the sense of anger many Indians feel. Edward McDaniel's poem that was used as the introductory piece for the "Indian Stories" section speaks plainly of his anger at the loss of water and land, his frustration with people who "mess with the Res. [reservation]," and his hope of becoming the captain of the dancers.

McDaniel's poem—for the "public" that comprises Elk Creek—is a threatening, yet eloquent voice. It is a message that, outside of the publication, would not only not have been uttered in this way, and it also would not have been listened to. There were many instances in the book of such critiques, yet that was not the only message. Other students wrote directly to inform—to tell the whole community of Elk Creek what the dances, the traditions, and the culture of Grindstone are all about. Dee Swearinger's "The Great Big Head Dance" tells in detail about the most important dance on the Grindstone. For instance, she tells about the remarkable headdress, which signifies the "Big Head":

The headdress is made of tulies, feathers, and sticks. The big head was made out of poppies; there were not enough poppies to make the headdress, so they now use feathers. The headdress takes about 126 sticks to make it look really beautiful and full. The headdress looks like a big sticker bush. It takes the men one day to make just the headdress. The headdress weighs about 30 pounds. The men use goose feathers or any kind of white feathers to tie around the sticks. The use tulies for a place to put the sticks to make the head look real big. They get the tulies and cut them at the root underneath the water. They string the tulies and tie them together to make the headdress and the skirts.

The dances should be a national treasure, yet many of the non-Indian population of Elk Creek know little about the dance other than its name. Indian students at the school began to see the publication as an opportunity to argue for their traditions as a legitimate part in the community. Thus, there are essays about religious beliefs, the dances, and the roundhouse in the collection.

The publication project had some surprisingly far-reaching effects. Partly due to the new status accorded the reservation, Walser argued successfully for a release day for faculty, staff, and students so that the dancers from the Grindstone could demonstrate the celebratory dances to the school. For nearly everyone it was the first time that they had actually seen the Indian dancers, even though dances are open to the public. It also signaled a willingness on the part of the school to make some changes.

For individual students, too, the publication project seemed to make a difference. Dee Swearinger, the author of "The Great Big Head Dance" became the first Native-American woman to graduate from high school in at least eight years. Her brother Gale "Turk" not only graduated, but through a separate grant, returned to school as the first Native American aide. The publication was very warmly received by the whole community, despite the fact that many of the students' essays critiqued life in Elk Creek.

The publication did not solve problems between whites and Native Americans in Elk Creek. Poverty and despair continue at Grindstone, as in other parts of the Elk Creek area. Racism did not disappear, either, within the school or the community. It isn't within the power of the writing project, the school alone, or a single teacher, even a mighty one like Jo Walser, to make such changes. But *Merging Communities* successfully, if temporarily, pushed against the forces of racism by calling attention to the Indian students and their community. Its effects may be temporary, or so limited as to not matter at all. It is hard to tell. It isn't difficult for me to say that this was a good project, that it might have helped some students, that it might—with continued pressure

from Grindstone and sympathetic teachers and community members—
contribute to more substantive change in the community.

Imagining Coordinated Actions

The mainstreaming of basic writing, the work on standards by the Writing Across the Disciplines program, and the Elk Creek publication project have several features in common. Each worked rhetorically against a dominant ideology that limits access. Rodby argued directly against the basic idea that structures most curricula in writing, that literacy comes in context-free levels. She got national support when she needed it from conference presentations, yet she also worked hard at the local level, in teachers' meetings, with tutors, and in one-to-one talks with faculty and administrators. Wolf and Renfro subtly shifted an administrative command for setting standards to a discussion about the purposes of standards by slowly and carefully challenging ideologies of standards. The Writing Project publication challenged existing ideas about Indian students by creating a socially powerful forum for them to argue, inform, and disprove. In each case, ideologies that would have prevented access were challenged and, in some cases, partly transformed.

Additionally, these events—and the programs they represent—span the curriculum: the Writing Project works with K–12 teachers, the first-year composition program "greets" all freshmen, and the Writing Across the Disciplines program works with all levels and disciplines. This multilevel, multidisciplinary reach gives our efforts greater reach and more potential.

One of de Certeau's most famous phrases is that "practices exceed structures." He is claiming in that passage that *resistive* practices exceed *oppressive* structures. But the reverse is true, too. No small group of faculty, no matter how persistent, can "fix" the structures of the university so that students of color enter and are successful. We can eliminate first-year composition, but that doesn't solve the problem that most students of color don't even apply for college. We can work through the writing project to increase the number of students who see college as in their interest, but no WAD program can eliminate the subtle, and obvious, ways that racism excludes students once they are here.

Yet there is potential in imagining administrative work in writing programs as a series of coordinated, collaborative practices that open the discussions of academic disciplines to broader populations and extend meaningful relationship by establishing communications across traditional boundaries and by fighting oppressive institutional structures. Certainly, success will be limited in our lifetimes, and possibly the rate of change will be too slow for those too long excluded.

Chapter Five

Access and Classroom Practice

By describing the practices of writing program administrators as political action in the last chapter, I argued for an elaborated and somewhat altered version of the Gramscian notion of the war of position. Classroom teaching of composition is the most important part of this coordinated political action. Many composition teachers have written extensively about how and why teaching is a political activity. This research demonstrates the multiple and various manifestations of what political means in the classroom and the various ways that political is realized. Many of the claims that composition pedagogy is transformative, my own work included, have come under scrutiny. The profession has come to suspect claims of political transformation. These stem, I believe, from a more sophisticated understanding of domination, one explored in the last chapter as hegemonic and not directly oppressive.

In this chapter, I would like to begin by specifying a series of standards for teaching writing that resist the historically powerful oppositions of standards and access. These standards, since they seek to work on history, are themselves subject to changes in history. They are contingent upon the local needs, conditions, and qualities of specific student bodies, and specific programs. They are aimed at reducing the crisis of access in higher education through critical consciousness and by exploring texts and contexts that have in the past worked to increase the freedoms of oppressed people. No one reading this book should mistake the argument of this book for an argument against high expectations for students. I am arguing *against* the persuasive power of the reasoning that says access is contingent on meeting acontextual standards of the academy. I am arguing *for* contingencies that see standards critically in a relationship with social and political change. The former removes standards from teachers' judgments, the latter depends on teachers to make judgments.

As a tentative move toward describing standards that would work for access in the teaching contexts I explore in this chapter, I offer the following writing standards as a framework:

- writing that interrogates cultural/political commonplaces, that refuses to repeat clichéd explanations for poverty, racism, sexism, homophobia, and all the other diseases of our society;
- writing that willingly explores and embodies conflicts, that isn't afraid to enter into the messy contradictions of our world;
- writing that critiques institutional inequities, especially in the immediate context of the classroom, the writing program, the department, the university, but also in the institutions that have played an important role in our students' lives;
- writing that demonstrates successful practices of resistance, that seeks historical evidence for possibilities and promise;
- writing that complexly addresses complex issues, that doesn't seek safety in simplicity;
- writing that seeks a wide audience by respecting the dignity of others, yet has the courage to stand against those who are unjust;
- writing that self-consciously explores the workings of its own rhetoric;
- in short writing that seeks to reduce the violence of inequality— the social forces that prevent access.

The three sections that follow discuss classroom practices and student work that usefully broach the issues of access explored in the earlier chapters of this book. They represent both a variety of approaches to teaching for access, and also my own progression of ideas during the last several years.

I. The No-Contact Zone

Like many compositionists, I was impressed by Mary Louise Pratt's conception of multicultural education as "contact zone" in "The Arts of the Contact Zone." She concludes that article with a call for more discussion: "We are looking for the pedagogical arts of the contact zone" (1991, 40). She also names some of those arts, many of which are forms of writing:

> These will include, we are sure, exercises in storytelling, and in identifying with the ideas, interests, histories, and attitudes of others; ex-

periments in transculturation and collaborative work and in the arts of critique, parody, and comparison (including unseemly comparisons between elite and vernacular cultural forms); the redemption of the oral; ways for people to engage with suppressed aspect of history (including their own histories); ways to move *into and out of* rhetorics of authenticity; ground rules for communication across lines of difference and hierarchy that go beyond politeness but maintain mutual respect; a systematic approach to the all-important concept of *cultural mediation.* (1991, 40)

That Pratt's conception of the classroom as a contact zone was picked up by so many composition theorists so quickly (see Bartholomae, Lu, Miller, Harris, for examples) attests to the fit between the contact zone and our own sense of what multicultural classrooms are like. Part of the appeal, no doubt, was that it replaced the ideas of community that the profession abandoned in the early 1990s, after the publication of Harris' "The Idea of Community in the Study of Writing." I found the metaphor useful because it allowed for conflict, history, and power as defining features. The contact zone refers "to social spaces where cultures meet, clash, grapple with each other, often in contexts of highly asymmetrical relations of power, such as colonialism, slavery, or their aftermath as they are lived out in many parts of the world today" (Pratt 1991, 34).

I often teach first-year composition courses at my university that are tagged as "multicultural." These courses were initiated at the joint request of some composition faculty and students of color following a student-organized conference on Indian education. Since students of color comprise a small minority on my campus, many felt alienated in their classes. Multicultural sections of composition were designed to attract more students of color and reduce the sense of alienation that some students felt.

Since the student population of the classroom was multicultural, I wondered if "the contact zone" could work as a curricular strategy to help students write about cultural difference. So I set up a series of assignments that would provide students with information about each other and a theoretical framework (Pratt's) that would help them conceive of themselves as "grappling." I began by assigning Clifford Geertz's "Notes on a Balinese Cockfight" for a common text that considers questions of culture. After presentations and class discussions on that text, I assigned the following essay (which is very similar to Bartholomae and Petrosky's assignment in *Ways of Reading*):

Write an essay about the significance of a "game" in your own culture. This game could be anything from shopping to partying to family ceremonies. This essay should include a detailed description of the "game" and an interpretation of its significance in the culture. Use Geertz's description and analysis of the Balinese Cockfight as an example.

Although some students had difficulty with finding the "significance" of their game in their drafts, on the whole these essays turned out very nicely. We worked hard on revisions and by the end of a few weeks, each student had a polished draft that went into a student publication titled, "The Contact Zone." The students edited the complete text and decided chapter headings and the order of the essays. We then read Pratt's essay, which the students found difficult. So we talked about the difficulty, her audience, and the context of her argument. Most of the students, while they may not have understood the context of all Pratt's remarks (for example the context of "linguistic utopias" that she was writing against), got the gist of her article. So I assigned the following paper:

> Read our class book. Look for patterns, similarities, and conflicts. Then write about what you see. This essay asks you to write about the cultures that make up our class. How are they similar? How are they different? Mary Louise Pratt says that contact zones are "social spaces where cultures meet, clash, and grapple with each other." How is our class a contact zone?

What I hoped from this assignment was that students would recognize and write about difference in our classroom. There *was* difference. For example, a white student wrote about the ritual of driving to Tijuana to get drunk with his friends; a Latina student wrote about traditions of low-riding; another woman wrote about an exclusive summer camp; yet another wrote about the rituals of working at a fast-food restaurant. An enduring feature of the literacy history of the United States, according to Bizzell, is writing about cultural difference ("Contact Zone"). I sought to provide a rhetorical occasion for that kind of writing. I imagined that students would write about the effects of economic, gender, and racial difference on the ways that their cultural traditions evolved. In class, I modeled that kind of analysis by suggesting differences in social status and class among the essays.

Of course, students didn't write that. They wrote essays like Ray's, which was tellingly titled "All the Same." In his essay, Ray's main point was to show that although the student writers "came from different backgrounds," they all have "something in common." Here's what his take is on the diversity of the class:

> We all go through phases such as friends, rituals, problems, and going to the next level of life. We learn to stay together as one and bond as best friends forever. The T.J. Posse developed friendships that last forever when they went on the trip to Tijuana every month; Danielle and her best friends going on a senior trip to Cancun, Mexico; Ying and his boys causing problems with they spit ball fights, all stay together as one. We gain nicknames such as D.O.C., Longball, 2.0, and the Irie Boys. Thus, when we form our groups, we unite as one. . . . We are like each other, but just don't want to admit it.

Ray, as one of three African Americans in class, was faced with significant rhetorical challenges. In addition to being African American, he
was also from New York and felt little in common with the other black
students who were from California. One of the issues that he talked
about in class was the difficulty that faced John in W. E. B. Du Bois' essay, "The Coming of John," and one that John Ogbu writes about extensively: the conflict between educational success and African American
community life. Ray told the story of going to a mostly white school in
California and becoming best friends with whites:

> I was dressing like them. I was acting like them. Everyday when I sent
> home, the Blacks in my town couldn't relate with me. They called me
> a sell out (hanging out with the other race) but I didn't care. I knew I
> was black and not white, but we were friends, not for the colors.
>   Whenever I came home from college, everything back home
> changed. I related better now with my neighbor friends, but in their
> eyes I am still a sell out. . . .
>   The story of John had me thinking about my culture and the thing
> that's going on in the world today. In some people's eyes back home I
> am lost in the white world. I am not lost. I know what's going on in
> our society. I know there is racism . . . You must stand strong and
> get an education. Then you will have a say. . . . One day there will
> be peace, but not in our time. The main killer is that bad bug hate fly-
> ing around like a cold that is deadly, killing one another. We are killer
> people because there are differences, but really we are killing the en-
> tire race. There are drive by shootings, murders, rapes, you name it,
> every race has got it. . . . it's a context of power, greed, and who could
> destroy who and take over. There will never be peace as long as there
> is hate, greed, and power. One day there will be peace, that is when
> no one is left.

When Ray was part of a group presentation on urban blacks, he dramatically told the story of being called "whitey" by his neighborhood
friends for (he said) going to a white school. He rolled up his sleeve for
the class and showed his arm, and with some anger asked, "Does that
look white to you?"

It was a complex and polysemic gesture in some ways. At once,
Ray asserted both his identity as "black," his independence from urban
stereotypes that overwhelm mainstream culture's perception of black
males, and obliquely, his determination to belong to this group, the
classroom, the university. It was an assertion of difference and same-
ness at the same time.

It isn't surprising to go back to Ray's "Contact Zone" paper and understand why he so relentlessly asserted that the class was "all the same."
It wasn't a statement of truth; it was an argument, an argument that is
in the same context as his discussion of hate. My point is that achievement in a multicultural class is a complicated judgment. In my first

reading of this essay, I felt like Ray was uncritical, ready to embrace an unthinking unity, an old-fashioned melting pot idea. A closer reading led me to see that "difference" remained present (though usually, perhaps appropriately, subordinated) through his essay. Finally, a reading that saw Ray's Contact Zone essay in the context of his other concerns convinces me that Ray is rhetorically sophisticated, writing the careful line between affiliation and difference, writing to achieve both access and change. I still believe students need to write more directly about difference and conflict because it may help us sort out the difficult problems our country faces. This particular assignment, for Ray and for other students, however, failed to produce that discourse because of the tightrope of belongingness and difference that students of color often have to walk.

After thinking about Ray's paper and the difficulty he faced, I revised my course to include a stronger sense of history in the exploration of writing about difference. I was particularly interested in demonstrating to all students, but particularly to students of color, the ways in which writing about the contact zone was a continuing concern of our history. As Patricia Bizzell has suggested in "Contact Zones and English Studies" one way to imagine the rhetorical studies in the United States is to imagine a history of writers who have "grappled with the pervasive presence of difference in American life" (1994, 168). One of the difficulties that writers like Ray, Leon, and other African Americans face is that the construction of academic studies marginalizes, misrepresents, or neglects their history. This neglect requires each new generation to take on the heavy role of trailblazer. My composition class seeks to show that people of color have used writing as a means of intervening in oppressive political structures for a long time: writing against slavery, lynchings, genocide, Jim Crow, and other atrocities. Instead of feeling like they have to create a new voice to argue with, students of color find themselves within a tradition, a sturdy rhetorical stance. What I have in mind is the kind of "assurance" that Jackie Royster writes about as she researched the intellectual traditions of black women writers:

> A historical view of the ways in which African American women have used writing assures us that we are not looking at just a struggle for basic literacy. . . . They have established themselves not just as readers and writers but as master artisans and visionaries, that is, they belong to the central traditions of the literate world at its best. (Royster 1990, 104)

This history is especially urgent, I believe, for African American students. My explanation of this urgency requires examining the ways that teaching writing to African-America students has erased this history of literacy and posited instead a deficit.

No Deficits: a Detour

The myth that African Americans suffer from a linguistic of cultural deficiency of one kind or another has doggedly hampered any efforts to change composition curriculum. One of the results of this persistent myth is that the history of nonliterary writing has been obscured. One of the most nefarious ways that African American student discourse has been neutralized, demeaned, and diminished is ill-constructed dichotomies of speech and writing. Deficit theory was first demolished by linguists who studied speech. The most famous was William Labov, whose 1969 treatise, "The Logic of Non-Standard English" attacks two notions of deficit theory, "verbal deprivation" and "cultural deprivation." Labov's work, supported by other linguists including Fasold, Wolfram, and others, clearly demonstrated the logic, complexity, and efficacy of African American speech. Further studies, such as Geneva Smitherman's *Talkin' and Testifyin'* and Thomas Kochman's *Black and White Styles in Conflict* confirmed and elaborated on Labov's work. Speech, then, was rescued from deficit theories.

At this time, the early 1970s, composition research had done very little research on written discourse by African American students. "Early" scholars of composition in the modern era, like Shaughnessy, used the research on Black English Vernacular as a way, not just of respecting linguistic competence (like most linguists, "linguistic" meant speech), but as a way of understanding the written discourse of African American basic writers as a deficiency. "Dialect interference" became a strong term for the "problems" of African American student writing. Because these two terms have been used together for over twenty years in our professional vocabulary, we need to stand back from them to see the actual strangeness of their pairing. For "dialect" to "interfere" with writing, one must first of all imagine a conflicting relationship between speech and writing. Note that this relationship of conflict does not assume the same potency with any other ethnic group. White Southerners, some of whose dialect resembles Black English Vernacular, are not routinely charged with dialect interference. The research used to demolish deficit theories of speech was then used to create new deficit theory for African American student writing.

This move was supported by research into orality and literacy that originated in the description of the cultural changes in classical Greece after the introduction of writing. In an influential article first published in the journal of the Associated Department of English, Walter Ong ties together the research of classical orality and literacy with the language use of African American students. I'd like to take a closer look at the premises of this piece, especially the ways in which Ong constructs the "orality" of urban African American students. Ong's claim is that "orality" is not just a linguistic category; it is not just a way of using language.

It is cultural, a "state of consciousness" ([1975]1987, 47), and for Ong that means several things, but above all it means cognitive differences. Orality comes in many varieties, among them "primary" and "secondary." Primary orality, according to Ong, is "the pristine orality of mankind untouched by writing or print" (49). The cognitive/cultural world of pristine orality excludes "analytically sequential, linear organization of thought" (47) and excludes the ability to write an autobiography, or the type of autobiography that is "closely plotted in the sense in which Greek drama is closely plotted, with a steady rush of complex action to climax, peripeteia or reversal, and subsequent falling action and denouement" (47–48). Orality is "formulaic or rhapsodic" (50).

Most readers are now familiar with the many criticisms of Ong's and others' version of "the great divide" between oral and literate cultures (see Daniell). I want to explore here the specific consequences of this claim when applied to African American writers. Ong's case for the "orality" of urban blacks rests on two amazingly weak examples. The first is a question and response between an instructor and a "black inner-city student." The instructor asks, "What do you think of Nixon's action in Cambodia?" and the student responds, "I wouldn't vote for that turkey. He raised his own salary." Ong sees evidence of primary oral culture by assuming that this answer is "purely emotional, not at all 'logical'"(50). In a patronizing rereading of this conversation, Ong shows how this response "is perfectly intelligent." Ong claims that the student was "unconcerned with analysis" because in a primary oral culture "intensive analysis is not practiced, not even thought of." He also claims that since oral cultures polarized good and evil, the student's answer was a good one because he stated clearly that Nixon was evil.

The second example of an oral culture is even less persuasive:

> I was visiting the class of a graduate teaching assistant who was teaching writing. In one of the chairs sat a young man who, as I found subsequently, was from the highly oral inner-city black ghetto. He was very attentive, trying hard. But he had no textbook with him, and it was immediately apparent that he did not feel at all disadvantaged by this fact. . . . (Ong [1975] 1987, 51)

Ong goes on to compare this student to one of Plato's boys, where "education consists of identification, participation, getting into the act, feeling affinity with the culture's heroes, getting 'with it'—not in analysis at all" (51). This heavy—and damning—conclusion is based on his observation that one of the students, possibly having forgotten his book, tried to act as if he were interested (perhaps because Ong was observing the teaching assistant that day).

Ong's student, Thomas Farrell, has also used this argument, although he refers to urban African American students not as from a "primary oral culture" but from a "residually oral culture," where people can read and write (at least rudimentally) but are still dominated by an oral frame of mind. Much has been written about the ways in which Ong and Farrell have appropriated classical studies of orality and literacy, and forceful arguments have been presented that convincingly refute the distinctions that characterize Ong's discussion of orality and literacy (see Heath, Daniell, and Scribner and Cole). I will refer readers to those discussions. I would like to add to them the serious criticism that neither Ong nor Farrell has ever presented convincing evidence that urban black communities are either primarily or residually oral in the sense that Ong and Farrell mean.

My argument does not deny or minimize scholarship that has proven that African American oral discourse styles are distinctive, interesting, and evidence of a culture that values talk, as Smitherman, Baugh, Kochman, Labov, and others have shown. Nor does it refute the research demonstrating that African Americans have distinct rhetorical traditions, as explored by Valerie Balester in *Cultural Divide* or Kermit Campbell. Those claims are beyond reproach. However, are these language practices evidence of an oral culture, similar to Greece before writing? Is it evidence of a culture that doesn't practice analysis or can only crudely dichotomize good and evil?

In actual student writing by black teenagers, some researchers have shown that dialect has very little to do with the errors that black student writers make and that these writers generally make the same errors that other students do. Geneva Smitherman's research into the Black English Vernacular in the writing of black teenagers on the National Assessment of Educational Progress (NAEP) written examination confirms this point of view. Smitherman's research shows that features of Black English, especially the deletion of the copula, the deletion of the *-ed* morpheme, the *-s* morpheme on third person, and the *IT*-expletive are all declining in samples on the NAEP assessment. In fact, for all except the *-ed* morpheme and the *-s* morpheme, features of Black English in written compositions among black teenagers occur at statistically insignificant levels. Jane Zeni and Joan Krater Thomas confirm Smitherman's thesis with a different population, concluding, "'Black Dialect' is clearly not the key issue for African American writers in this suburban community" (1990, 25).

Consider the following essay from my campus:

> My past history of English was not so great. But I guess the main thing about it, is that I hate to write, and read. The only time I see myself doing it is when it is required in school.
>
> When I move to California, the English class I had was not so bad, because it didn't have a lot of written assignments. Also my English teacher Mr. Palm was so funny, that he made me want to be there every day.

> The senior English I had was very hard, which I barely past with
> a D. When I was here for summer bridge, a lot of my teachers told
> me that my grammer was bad. One of my instructors said that I was
> around to much street language, which was understandable from the
> back ground I came from. So I hope this lets you know about the
> things I need help on in English.

This is an unedited first draft; there are about seven mistakes: homonym
misspellings (*to* for *too* and *past* for *passed*); *grammer* for *grammar;* four
extra commas; one *d* left off the past tense; and one compound word,
background, separated into two. Only one of these errors could *possibly*
be related to "street language" and that's the *d* on *move*. Given that he
used the *d* on *required*, the chances are that even this error was a simple
omission and not a result of dialect interference.

We can see, however, the ease with which the oral/literate dichot-
omy is employed. A teacher—a well-meaning teacher—seeks a way of
telling the writer what she truly believes. First, he has writing problems;
his teachers believe his "grammer is bad." Second, he needs an explanation that will help him turn his attention to writing. So the teacher
uses the concept of "dialect interference" to tell him that he needs to
work on his writing. What would happen? The diagnosis is wrong, so
Bobby's ability to understand how street language impairs his writing
won't improve it. It will remain a mysterious ailment. The diagnosis
also recreates an institutional opposition that has worked against African Americans from the beginning of composition instruction. That is,
from the student's point of view, the language of the street damages his
ability to write the language of the academy. For this writer, as for most
students, the language of the street is not a collection of discourse forms
or lexical items, it is a social identity. Third, and most troubling because
much is lost, the analysis of oral interference suppresses much more
important questions about the student's writing. Why does he hate to
read and write in school? "Senior English" was not such a great time.
What went on? He doesn't say. What does "schooled" writing mean to
Bobby? What *could* it mean? What are the potentials for reading and
writing that Bobby has not imagined?

Unfortunately there was little corresponding work to Labov and
Smitherman on the literacy habits of African Americans in everyday
life that would argue against the literacy deficit theory until the 1980s.
Then, ethnographies began to contradict the image of the "literacy deficit." Most well-known is Shirley Brice Heath's previously cited *Ways
with Words*. Heath documents carefully the various literacy practices of
the African American community, Trackton. One could make the case,
as Heath does, that these practices are not the practices of the school,
but one could not make the argument that Trackton lacks literate habits.
Heath documents children as young as three reading environmental

print. She also gives us an extended account of Sunday church services, where oral and written uses of language merge in a performance (for another, more extended treatment of the African American sermon, see Moss). Heath makes the point that written language in Trackton is almost always attended by oral discussion of it, and she also makes the point that the sermon's use of call and response is formulaic. She sums up the uses of literacy in Trackton:

> . . . the written word is for negotiation and manipulation—both serious and playful. Changing and changeable, words are the tools performers use to create images of themselves and the world they see. (1983, 235)

Her point, however, is that these uses of literacy do not prepare Trackton residents for the uses of literacy at school. On one level, it seems like an obvious point; the world of the black church and the world of the mainstream school are far apart. But it is not Heath's point that the *world* of Trackton does not prepare them for success in school. Her focus is specifically on language, that *language* use does not prepare them for success in school. To make this point is to make two overlapping assumptions: (1) that the language styles of the Trackton children remain doggedly with them even as they enter the new context of school, and/or (2) the language use of the Trackton residents is inappropriate for school. These assumptions tend to totalize language use by imagining that no—or few—contexts in the students' lives prepare them for school. For instance, it is hard to imagine why constant talk about text wouldn't better prepare students for school than the silent reading habits of the mainstream families. Although it is clear that Trackton residents do not do as well in school, Heath's specific focus on language style excludes other powerful explanatory possibilities, including economic differences, racism, and the differing amount of social capital that schooling represents for different communities.

Even more relevant to refuting the literacy deficit theory for African Americans is Denny Taylor and Catherine Dorsey-Gaines' remarkable ethnography *Growing up Literate*, which studies the relationship between home literacy and school in urban African American families. They found that these families, sometimes in the worst of economic times, remained committed to teaching their children to read and write. They also found that all kinds of literate practices punctuated their daily lives, from complex and technical forms for assistance from social service agencies, to schoolwork supported by home environments, to reading for pleasure, which Taylor and Dorsey-Gaines say is "a prominent feature in each of the homes we visited" (1988, 138). One of the most important points that Taylor and Dorsey-Gaines make is that "sociohistorical" reading and writing was an important aspect of the literacy practices of inner-city African Americans. Residents of the homes studied in this ethnography read "academic" prose, especially prose related to civil rights, African American identity, and the historic struggle of black people against slavery and racism. The list of titles that Jerry, one of their research subjects, presents to the researchers is impressive in its range (Bettelheim to Dostoevsky to Baldwin) and the predominance of nonfiction-analytical writing. Taylor and Dorsey-Gaines' evidence directly contradicts Ong and Farrell's claims.

II. Historicizing Student Writers

These images of literate activity in African American communities need to be obvious in composition classrooms. Examples of powerful writing for social action make the point to students that the opposition between "literacy" and the "academy" is not one of discourse form, nor is the opposition simply "oral" versus "literate" or "street" versus "school." Instead it is the struggle for equality and access, and African Americans have used literacy as a tool in that struggle from the day they set foot in America. Historical examples make the case twice over: Not only are African Americans literate, but they also have been for a long time.

The assignment below seeks to reconnect students with a literate history, to engage students with the process of recapturing the literate strengths of those with whom they wish to stand. For African American students, this assignment has been particularly effective.

The History Assignment

This assignment focuses on a nonfiction writer of your choice who wrote before 1930. Choose someone whose writing is meaningful to you, whose history is somehow connected to your own. It may be someone you really admire or it may be someone you feel you need to know more about.

The idea is for you to find someone that *you* admire, a writer that you are interested in. It could be someone very local to your situation, a great-grandparent, for instance, or a community leader. It does not have to be someone who primarily identifies him- or herself as a writer. As we have discussed in class, writing occurs in many different professions, life styles, and cultures. If you do choose an unpublished writer, make sure you have access to his or her writing.

The first step is to choose an author and select short essays, newspaper or newsletter articles, book chapters, or journal/diary entries to use in your essay. You should check out or copy this **primary source** (that is, the author's own writing) and bring it to class. Be prepared to make a short presentation about the author and the piece you have selected to your group members. On this day, you should hand in a rough draft that tells about the author's writing. Answer the following questions:

1. What is the author most concerned about. What issue? What event? or What?

2. What is your response? What do you think about the author now that you have done some reading?

3. What do you need to know about surrounding culture and history now so you can really understand what the author is writing about?

Next, you will be expected to do some research that answers question 3 above. This research will involve **secondary sources,** sources that show you the historical context of your writer, the times and events of his or her life. These sources can be history textbooks, biographies, articles about the author's life. You'll be on your own finding these, but we'll talk about some ways to find and use these sources. Make sure you get all the documentation you need for these sources, including author, exact quotation, publisher, date, and page number. Write down the call number (if it is a book) so that you can find the book again if you need to. Write a draft of a paper that seeks to understand how this author's work fit into (or worked against) a particular set of historical circumstances.

Finally, I would like you to review your own writing during the past semester and chart some similarities and differences between your writing and the author you chose. How are your texts alike or different from the writer you studied?

My aim in this assignment was for students to find someone whom they could cite who was from the tradition within which they could imagine themselves. It is, in some senses, a traditional academic research paper. Yet for my students, this assignment often marks a turning point, the paper that students routinely cite as their most significant work of the semester. The choices students make are varied and multidisciplinary: sports writers, the inventor of the calculator, Booker T. Washington, David Walker, Dorothy Parker, W. E. B. Du Bois, Ida B. Wells.

For instance, Kay's work shows the sense of relevance that students find reading their author. Kay was an older African American who was open about her anger toward white supremacy and her suspicion of white people. She chose to write about W. E. B. Du Bois and began her paper by citing the famous passage in "Of Our Spiritual Strivings" from *The Souls of Black Folk:*

the Negro is a sort of seventh son, born with a veil, and gifted with second-sight in this American world,—a world which yields him no true self-consciousness, but only lets him see himself through the revelation of the other world. It is a peculiar sensation, the double-consciousness, this sense of always looking at one's self through the eyes of other, of measuring one's soul by the tape of a world that

looks on in amused contempt and pity. One ever feels his twoness,
an American, a Negro; two souls, two thoughts, two unreconciled
strivings . . . ." (Du Bois [1903] 1989, 3)

She was surprised, as many students are, by this single most prescient
writer of the twentieth century. She recast Du Bois' words as her own
feelings, then goes on to construct a history for them:

> From that moment on my eyes began to water because he touched a
> part of my heart that has shielded my feelings of hatred towards the
> white race. It's no secret to anyone that knows me on a personal level
> that I am very sensitive towards black and white issues. And some-
> times my views tend to be biased and one-sided. Nevertheless, I still
> try to understand and look at the whole picture before I express my
> views.
>   Anyway, Du Bois is speaking from the heart and souls of many of
> my black brothers and sisters. The emancipation proclamation, the year
> we were considered a free race and when we were finally give the per-
> mission to vote by whites, is only the beginning of our so-called free-
> dom. Our minds are still enslaved. In my opinion we are still caught
> up trying to be other than what we are; Black People.

This last part, the commentary on the "pain" of double-consciousness,
becomes a theme of Kay's paper. As central evidence in that argument
Kay cites the wonderful essay in *Souls*, "The Coming of John." Du Bois'
essay concerns a black man from the South who goes North to school.
Upon returning South, he finds himself changed and unfit for his former
life. Kay cites the following conversation between John and his sister:

> "John," she said, "does it make every one—unhappy when they
> study and learn lots of things?"
>   He paused and smiled. "I'm afraid it does," he said.
>   "And, John, are you glad you studied?"
>   "Yes," came the answer slowly, but positively. (Du Bois [1903]
> 1989, 171)

Kay's commentary on this passage is instructive:

> What this passage means to me is that the truth to the whole story
> must be sought out and understood, even if it's bad. You can't under-
> stand if you just know bits and pieces of the information. Especially if
> the pieces of information you do know are basically polished and forced
> into your subconscious in such a way that it bares no significance or
> meaning at all.

Kay's engagement with Du Bois was strong and forceful. It triggered for
her yet another examination of her educational history, especially the
ways that racial issues were suppressed. The sense that somehow she
and Du Bois—as writers—were involved in the same project is under-

scored by the following conclusion: "Du Bois made me feel sad and happy at the same time. The reason I say this is because he expressed a lot of the same feelings I have, but on the other hand, I was kind of sad because everything he talked about is very true today in 1992."

Ricky's paper on David Walker revealed a careful reading of Walker and his context. Most people are familiar with Du Bois, but few know David Walker's *Appeal in Four Articles*, a remarkable text written in 1836 and discussed briefly in Chapter 2. Although Ricky had earlier cited rapper KRS-one as a philosopher who argued that schools need to teach Black history, he was fairly reluctant to read Walker or choose somebody else. As he said, "I have a lack of interest toward history." Despite this, Ricky's paper showed that he read both Walker and the secondary sources thoughtfully.

> David Walker is an interesting writer. I hesitated towards constructing a research paper on him, but found myself really engaged in reading his work. In response to the *Appeal*, I gathered that David Walker was basically concerned with the black's suffering, dealing with ways to unite Blacks to defeat oppression. . . . I read about a man that concerned with making a change and determined to make that change with the help of God.

Walker's text is not easy to read; it's full of biblical references, extended syllogisms, and references to the current political scene. Yet there was no doubt that Ricky got it. While Ricky's analysis of Walker's text itself was impressive, most interesting was the parallel between KRS-one, the rapper, and Walker that Ricky made. Ricky noted that KRS-one advocated knowing Black history in order to make social change. After writing about Walker, Ricky said that he understood more what KRS-one was saying.

For Tina, the relationship between her writing and the tradition she chose to write about was clear. Tina, like virtually all of the students I have cited thus far in this chapter, would have been placed in the lowest section of basic writing had we maintained the program. She began my course tentatively. In her portfolio cover letter, she wrote: "At the beginning of the school year I thought I wrote papers like a 6th grader." Tina would fit the stereotype of an urban African American, "at-risk" student. She lacked confidence in her writing at first, and wrote, well, like a sixth grader. With each new task, however, she began to write more complexly and ambitiously. She had been told by her high school teacher not to write about more than one idea at a time. In conference, she complained about how difficult it was to write about only one idea when she had so many ideas in her head at once. I asked her to write about more than one idea. She said then her paper would be disorganized, and I responded, "I dare you."

Her next paper was indeed organized and dealt with a series of ideas regarding the cultural image of the rap group Arrested Development. The next paper was even stronger and more sophisticated. However, it was the history paper where Tina excelled. She wrote easily the best paper in the class, and one of the best papers I have ever received. Her topic was the work of Ida B. Wells. In order to make obvious the literacy history of African Americans, I bring texts to students that I think will capture their interest. I gave Ricky a copy of David Walker's *Appeals* (among other texts) and I suggested Ida B. Wells for Tina. These texts and other nonfictional historical texts by African Americans are less a presence in composition classrooms than texts by Alice Walker, Toni Morrison, or Richard Wright. Yet for student writers writing nonliterary texts, who better than Wells or Walker to demonstrate the importance of the "critique" as social action in the lives and histories of African Americans?

Tina's paper made a number of important points about Wells. She noted that Wells' compulsion to speak and write strongly was so powerful that she made few friends. She also noted Wells' early feminism, and that her criticism included black men. Tina's own work—the best of it—displayed similar characteristics. She saw in Wells' work a precursor to her own. In her cover letter for her portfolio, she writes:

> I believe my best writing of the semester was my research paper on Ida B. Wells. . . . I believe I really got into that paper because she was a lot like myself. She stood for what she believed in regardless of the consequences. She was a strong and determined Black women . . . , even at a time when Black women didn't have many rights.

Tina's success involved more than writing a good paper about Ida B. Wells; it involved her reconception of research and academic prose as viable and powerful forms of discourse for the social agenda of Black women, herself included.

The problem the assignment seeks to redress—the failure of education to help students of color construct a literacy tradition—sometimes becomes a problem in the assignment itself. Both Kay and Ricky remarked that "history" wasn't something they were particularly interested in doing. Kay was more specific: "You can't understand if you just know bits and pieces of the information. Especially if those pieces of information you do know are polished and forced into your subconscious in such a way that it bares no significance or meaning at all." "Polished" information "forced" into a mind is a frightening image, but one that the students have a difficult time giving up even if they are the ones responsible for writing the history. The work of the teacher, in this context, is to make historical texts by people of color available and compelling.

III. Sharpening the Edge:
Resistance and Critique

In many ways, Tina's paper on Ida B. Wells resembles a very good research paper of the type that has been written in first-year composition for many years. A cynical way to imagine her success in my class is that she learned to conform to the discourse standards in the university, standards that I've argued in this book have been used traditionally to deny access to students of color. She would be, then, one of the exceptions—one of those few students who make it and serve as an exemplar of the institution's fairness to all. I doubt whether Tina would see it that way. The point, as I see it, is that rather than conforming with an oppressive institution, Tina placed herself within a tradition of African American women intellectuals who together have resisted sexist and racist actions to silence them. This is the intellectual tradition that Royster cites as a supreme example of resistance: "the claiming of the status of tradition for black women's intellectualism is an act that goes radically against the tide. It is an act of empowerment. The power comes from having access to what Deirdre David calls 'intellectual ancestry'" (Royster 1990, 106).

William, a student who also wrote "traditional" academic papers, wrote keenly and self-consciously about the relationship of academic work and cultural resistance in his writing. The first sentence of his first paper reads: "But people find ways to subvert." William selected this quotation from the assigned reading, Chapter 4 of Ralph Cintron's *Angels' Town: Chero Way, Gang Life, and the Rhetorics of the Everyday.* For William, as well as for many other African American students who have faced that variety of deficit theories discussed earlier in this chapter, "subversion" means careful, critical, academic prose and a rigorously intellectual stance.

The central metaphor for William's subversion emerged from this paper, which asked students to do a cultural studies analysis of a wall in their room, modeled after Cintron's brilliant analysis of Valerio's wall in *Angels' Town.* William began his essay describing the representations of his success in high school football:

> my walls are filled with pictures, newspaper write-ups, plaques, and my game jersey. 'Each shape skillfully manipulated by some overwhelming bad luck or American culture.' That culture says that because I am Black I should be a great athlete, hands down. The most damaging evidence of that claim is my "collection" of college scouting letters.

William's insertion of the quotation from Cintron ("Each shape skillfully manipulated by some overwhelming bad luck or American culture"), and his assertion that the scouting letters are the "most damaging evidence" surprise and complicate his analysis of the wall. William was recruited by several colleges for his football abilities. These recruitment letters, he says, are important to him: "I was probably more excited than anyone to know that colleges wanted me to play ball for them." Yet at the same time, he calls them "a slap in the face" because they suppress his academic identity because of cultural stereotypes:

> One perspective is not all that my wall holds. Stating a stereotype, yet showing my dreams, is what my wall is all about. At one point in my life I wanted to participate in sports beyond the collegiate level. With the letters that I received, my dreams seemed to be within reach. "But people find ways to subvert," and upon the reception of my first letter of academic acceptance, I slowly broke away from that dream.

Imagine for a moment, the kind of determination it would take to resist your own dreams—and the scholarships attached to them—in order to reconstruct an identity that American culture suppresses. His agency is underscored by the fact that William displays the "insults" on his wall for his daily perusal.

There is no doubt after reading William's work that subversion is demonstrated by intellectual and academic achievement. Yet, it is impossible, reading William's work to conceive of his achievement in my class as simply conformity to academic rules of order. Take, for instance, his analysis of the Jaime Foxx Show, where William's central claim is that the Jaime Foxx Show is pleasurable to Black viewers because it "fills a void" by representing Black young people in a positive light. As he says, "none of the younger cast ended up be pregnant, involved with gangs or hooked on drugs." His conclusion stresses the efforts of African Americans to resist the limitations put on them by American culture:

> I have a void in my life, a small on[e] that every week or so needs to be filled. This void is somewhat small, but has a big impact on some decision that I make in everyday life. This void is filled with a false reality, a reality that shows we [Black people] are much more than athletes. More than gang members. We can achieve a status much higher than what society has taught us. The reality that is shown helps us to realize that there is much more out there for us to grab. The "Jaime Foxx Show" proves that there are intelligent role models out there. Even though these characters are fictional, they still offer a rare but true picture of the Black race.

William's achievement—and the achievement of Black intellectuals in history—is a precise, complex critique of white supremacy in its various forms and effects, including the effects on him personally. In a retrospective essay on his own papers, he says: "my papers show that I am partly trying to 'escape the world's grasp.'" From his refusal to accept the athletic recruitment to his constant focus on race and intellectual achievement, William tries to escape the grasp of a world that limits his possibilities as an athlete, a Black man, and an intellectual.

The achievements of the students in this chapter are "academic" and "intellectual." They are also, I argue, examples of student critical writing, the conscious and careful actions of intellectual students designed to resist the limiting and damaging practices that reduce the numbers of students of color in university. Students, as usual, show us the way.

Conclusion: Staying Around

Contact with students like Leon, Kay, Ricky, Tina, William, and others make it difficult to be entirely pessimistic about education. Not much else outside of the classroom, however, makes me cheerful about the future. Indeed, a good composition class, as important and powerful as we know it can be, takes its place among the array of classes—past and future—in each student's consciousness. That important and powerful experience can, within a few years, become a trivial pleasant memory. A composition class, even a very good one, does not alone provide access.

For political change to occur through educational institutions we need coordinated action. Students need many points of contact with writing instruction that respects their language and intelligence, so that, by accretion, learning to write becomes a means of access. K–12 teachers and higher education must understand each other's contexts and work together to insure the success of students of color. Outside of National Writing Project sites, which as powerful as they are, only reach a small minority of teachers, very little communication occurs between these two segments.

In addition to seeking alliances up and down the curriculum, composition courses must not be the only place in the curriculum where students' literacy is supported. Writing Across the Curriculum programs provide necessary and important contexts to improve the teaching of writing, yet these programs are hardly ever supported with solid funding. The program I described in Chapter 4 has since been reduced dramatically. Without changes in the way the writing is taught across campus, good writing programs will be misunderstood, isolated, and impotent. As Writing Across the Curriculum programs grow out of the first stage of sharing techniques like journals and other informal writing strategies, they can begin to challenge ideologies of literacy inherited from the Harvard model. Yet often, it is precisely at that point that the programs become most threatened in terms of funding and support.

The paucity of institutional support for composition may be the best explanation for why assessment practices in writing lag so desperately behind assessment theory. The recent Conference on College Composition and Communication statement on writing assessment that recommends against one-shot, timed, writing tests and against multiple-choice assessment is reasonable and well-argued. It is also not news to any composition teacher who reads professionally. Yet very few campuses anywhere in the nation escape the testing contradiction. One-shot placement and competency tests abound, and a surprising number of multiple-choice writing tests still exist.

The work necessary to dislodge these tests is enormous, as I indicated in Chapter 4. Their rootedness in the institution is defended on the ideas of acontextual standards as fair, equal, reasonable—ideas that in the history of the institution have become "common sense" and difficult to argue with. Yet over and over, the facts indicate that these tests typically fail nonnative speakers of English—African Americans, Latinos and other groups seeking access to higher education. To resist writing assessment requires persistence, numbers, and institutional clout. Aside from persistence, composition lacks the other two.

Within composition programs themselves, it is difficult to retain any institutional ground from which to work for change. In the crucial area of basic writing, where the need to eliminate no-credit courses is the most important step, many faculty simply do not have the institutional authority to argue for such changes. Too many administrators in writing programs are untenured and isolated, and too many are part-time and temporary. While the full-time faculty in composition has grown in the past ten years, it is nowhere near proportional to the numbers of courses in the curriculum. That leaves the full-time faculty responsible for more of the curriculum than they have power to shape. The collaboration described in Chapter 4 among full-time faculty always feels tenuous because there are so few of us. Composition faculty at my campus and across the country are often saddled with tremendous responsibilities, little authority, and few resources. This is why the politics of English departments are an issue of access.

So while the ways of working described in the last two chapters of this book remain possible, additional requirements are necessary: Greater material resources for composition programs in the form of tenure-track hires and fair workload assignments, and greater autonomy for making decisions about the nature of our programs, including assessment.

The image of work I wish to conclude with collapses the boundaries between students who work for their own place in higher education and composition teachers who wish to create institutions where access is valued. Watching successful students of color on my campus work provides a model of political action that composition professionals can learn from and emulate. My observations are personal, but they are also borne out by research on student persistence. I offer the following observations as guidelines for our work:

1. Stubborn persistence is necessary for change. Successful students of color simply give the impression that they will not ever go away until they succeed. Often, they simply exhaust the opposition. In my own Ph.D. program, for instance, the most successful students were the ones who refused to quit. Likewise, when composition specialists seek institutional changes, we need to adopt the attitude that change is inevitable and only a matter of time. We need to show up at every meeting with the expectation that now or the next time, we will prevail.

2. Success is often built on alliances across boundaries. Successful students of color develop friendships and alliances with each other, of course. And these are crucial. But additionally, they often develop relationships with librarians, tutors, older students, resident assistants in the dorms, and community members. The more numerous and broader the relationships students establish, the more likely they will be successful. It is easy, pleasant, and important to have close relationships with other professionals in composition. But we are doomed if we simply speak to ourselves. We need to become savvy about the local media, about holding intelligent and respectful conversations about composition with people who are uninformed. Despite the historic opposition of administration to faculty and to change, we need to watch for those administrators, especially the ones who remember teaching, who may be able to listen, learn, and help.

3. Students survive confrontations when they are prepared. The Boy Scouts had it right. Successful students of color on my campus are never shocked or stunned by educational racism. They have a broad range of prepared responses, from strategic and temporary silence to direct confrontation depending on their judgment of the context. Composition teachers and administrators should never be surprised when someone claims that students can't write a correct sentence and then blames composition teachers. Nor should they be surprised when a professor or administrator complains about falling levels of literacy and blames new students who "can't even speak English." The academy is no island of tolerance; it shares our culture's fear of change and difference. We need forceful, thoughtful, vigilant, and prepared responses to these challenges.

4. Survival is part of the process. Burnout and cynicism often stem from dashed expectations of change, the consequences of underestimating the power of institutions to reproduce themselves. Students who can gauge their own strength and strategically decide which battles are winnable and worth the energy are the ones who stay around. Reforming programs, challenging embedded tests,

fighting university and departmental practices can leave one demoralized and ineffective. Most of us in composition, because our programs and courses are undersupported, have, at one time or another, felt demoralized and ineffective. For most of us, it's a temporary feeling that signals that we have taken on too much with too high expectations for change. A degree of self-preservation helps.

Staying around is half the battle.

Works Cited

Anderson, James. 1988. *The Education of Blacks in the South, 1860–1935.* Chapel Hill: University of North Carolina Press.

Anderson, Worth, et al. 1990. "Cross-Curricular Underlife: A Collaborative Report on Ways with Academic Words." *College Composition and Communication* 41: 11–36.

Aronowitz, Stanley, and Henry A. Giroux. 1985. *Education Under Siege.* South Hadley, MA: Bergin and Garvey.

Baker, Houston A. 1984. *Blues, Ideology, and Afro-American Literature.* Chicago: University of Chicago Press.

Balester, Valerie M. 1993. *Cultural Divide.* Portsmouth, NH: Boynton/Cook.

Bartholomae, David. 1984. "Inventing the University." In *When a Writer Can't Write: Studies in Writer's Block and Other Composing Problems,* ed. Mike Rose, 134–165. New York: Guilford.

———. 1993. "The Tidy House: Basic Writing in the American Curriculum." *Journal of Basic Writing* 12(1) (Spring): 4–21.

Baugh, John. 1983. *Black Street Speech.* Austin: University of Texas Press.

Bennett, William. 1992. *The Devaluing of America: The Fight for Our Culture and Our Children.* New York: Summit.

Bereiter, Carl, and Siegfried Englemann. 1966. *Teaching Disadvantaged Children in the Preschool.* Englewood Cliffs, NJ: Prentice Hall.

Berlin, James. 1984. *Writing Instruction in Nineteenth-Century Colleges.* Carbondale, IL: Southern Illinois University Press.

Bizzell, Patricia. 1988. "Arguing About Literacy." *College English* 50: 141–153.

———. 1994. "Contact Zones and English Studies." *College English* 56: 163–169.

———. 1986. "What Happens When Basic Writers Come to College?" *College Composition and Communication* 37: 294–301.

Bloom, Allan. 1987. *The Closing of the American Mind.* New York: Simon and Schuster.

Brannon, Lil. 1995. "The Problem of National Standards." *College Composition and Communication* 46(3): 440–445.

Burke, Kenneth. 1969. *A Rhetoric of Motives.* Berkeley, CA: University of California Press.

Butchart, Ronald E. 1980. *Northern Schools, Southern Blacks, and Reconstruction: Freedmen's Education, 1862–1875*. Westport, CT: Greenwood.

Campbell, Kermit E. 1994. "The Signifying Monkey Revisited: Vernacular Discourse and African American Personal Narratives." *Journal of Advanced Composition* 14(2) (Fall): 463–473.

Child, Lydia Maria. [1865] 1968. *The Freedmen's Book*. New York: Arno Press.

Cintron, Ralph. 1997. Angels' Town: *Chero Way, Gang Life, and the Rhetoric of the Everyday*. Boston: Beacon Press.

Collins, James. 1989. "Hegemonic Practic: Literacy and Standard Language in Public Education." *Journal of Education* 171(2): 9–34.

Commission for the Review of the Master Plan for Higher Education. 1987. *The Master Plan Renewed*. Sacramento: State of California.

Conlin, Joseph R. 1993. Letter to the editor. *Enterprise-Record*. February 23, B4.

Connors, Robert J. 1991. "Rhetoric in the Modern University: The Creation of an Underclass." In *The Politics of Writing Instruction: Postsecondary*, eds. Richard Bullock and John Trimbur, 55–84. Portsmouth, NH: Boynton/Cook.

———. 1986. "The Rhetoric of Mechanical Correctness." In *Only Connect*, ed. Thomas Newkirk, 27–58. Portsmouth, NH: Boynton/Cook.

Cornelius, Janet Duitsman. 1991. *When I Can Read My Title Clear*. Columbia: University of South Carolina Press.

Daniell, Beth. 1986. "Against the Great Leap Theory of Literacy." *PRE/TEXT* 7: 181–193.

Davis, Charles T., and Henry Louis Gates, Jr. 1985. *The Slave's Narrative*. New York: Oxford University Press.

de Certeau, Michel. 1984. *The Practice of Everyday Life*. Berkeley, CA: University of California Press.

Deutsch, Martin, et al. 1967. *The Disadvantaged Child*. New York: Basic Books.

Douglas, Wallace. 1975. "Rhetoric for the Meritocracy." In *English in America*, Richard Ohmann, 97–132. New York: Oxford University Press.

D'Souza, Dinesh. 1991. *Illiberal Education: The Politics of Race and Sex on Campus*. New York: Vintage.

Du Bois, W. E. B. [1903] 1989. *The Souls of Black Folk*. New York: Bantam.

Farrell, Thomas. 1983. "I.Q. and Standard English." *College Composition and Communication* 34: 470–84.

Fasold, Ralph. 1972. *Tense Marking in Black English*. Arlington, VA: Center for Applied Linguistics.

Fulwiler, Toby, and Art Young, eds. 1990. *Programs That Work*. Portsmouth, NH: Boynton/Cook.

Gere, Anne Ruggles. 1994. "Kitchen Tables and Rented Rooms: The Extracurriculum of Composition." *College Composition and Communication* 45(1): 75–92.

Giroux, Henry. 1988. *Teachers as Intellectuals.* South Hadley, MA: Bergin and Garvey.

Graff, Gerald. 1987. *Professing Literature.* Chicago: University of Chicago Press.

Graff, Harvey. 1991. *The Literacy Myth.* New Brunswick, NJ: Transaction.

Gramsci, Antonio. 1971. *Selections from the Prison Notebooks.* New York: International.

Gross, Theodore. 1980. *Academic Turmoil.* New York: Anchor.

Harris, Joseph. 1989. "The Idea of Community in the Study of Writing." *College Composition and Communication* 40: 11–22.

———. 1997. *A Teaching Subject: Composition Since 1966.* Upper Saddle River, NJ: Prentice Hall.

Hayes, Janice. 1983. "The Development of Discursive Maturity in College Writers." In *The Writer's Mind,* eds. Janice Hayes et al., 127–144. Urbana: National Council of Teachers of Education.

Heath, Shirley Brice. 1981. "Towards an Ethnohistory of Writing in American Education." *Variation in Writing. Vol. 1 of Writing: The Nature, Development, and Teaching of Written Communication,* ed. Marcia Farr Whiteman, 25–46. Hillsdale, NJ: Lawrence Erlbaum.

———. 1983. *Ways with Words.* New York: Cambridge University Press.

Heller, L.G. 1973. *The Death of The American University with Special Reference to the Collapse of City College of New York.* New Rochelle, NY: Arlington House.

Herzberg, Bruce. 1991. "Composition and the Politics of the Curriculum." In *The Politics of Writing Instruction: Postsecondary,* eds. Richard Bullock and John Trimbur, 97–118. Portsmouth, NH: Boynton/Cook.

Holzman, Michael. 1989. "The Social Context of Literacy Education." In *Writing as Social Action,* eds. Marilyn M. Cooper and Michael Holzman, 133–140. Portsmouth, NH: Boynton/Cook.

Horner, Bruce. 1994. "Mapping Errors and Expectations for Basic Writing: From Frontier Field to Border Country." *English Education* 26: 29–51.

Jones, William. 1993. "Basic Writing: Pushing Against Racism." *Journal of Basic Writing* 12(1): 72–80.

Kochman, Thomas. 1981. *Black and White Styles in Conflict.* Chicago: University of Chicago Press.

Labov, William. 1972. *Language in the Inner City.* Philadelphia: University of Pennsylvania Press.

Lu, Min-Zhan. 1994. "Professing Multiculturalism: The Politics of Style in the Contact Zone." *College Composition and Communication* 45(4): 442–58.

———. 1991. "Redefining the Legacy of Mina Shaughnessy: A Critique of the Politics of Linguistic Innocence." *Journal of Basic Writing* 10(1) (Spring): 26–40.

Lunsford, Andrea. 1979. "Cognitive Development and the Basic Writer." *College English* 41: 38–46.

Lyons, Robert. 1980. "Mina Shaughnessy and the Teaching of Writing." *Journal of Basic Writing* 3: 307–15.

Merging Communities. 1990. Chico, CA: Northern California Writing Project.

Michaels, Sarah. 1986. "Narrative Presentations: An Oral Preparation for Literacy with First Graders." In *Social Construction of Literacy*, ed. Jenny Cook-Gumperz, 94–116. Cambridge: Cambridge University Press.

Miller, Richard. 1994. "Fault Lines in the Contact Zone." *College English* 56(4): 389–408.

Miller, Susan. 1991. *Textual Carnivals.* Carbondale, IL: Southern Illinois University Press.

Moss, Beverly J. 1994. "Creating a Community: Literacy Events in African-American Churches." In *Literacy Across Communities*, ed. Beverly Moss, 147–178. Cresskill, NJ: Hampton.

Myers, Miles. 1995. "Why Participate?" *College Composition and Communication* 46(3): 438–440.

National Center for Educational Statistics. 1996. "Scholastic Assessment Test (SAT) Scores." http://www.ed.gov/NCES/pubs/ce/c9622a01/html. (August 4, 1996).

National Council of Teachers of English. 1996. *Standards for the English Language Arts.* Urbana, IL: National Council of Teachers of English.

Ogbu, John. 1974. *The Next Generation.* New York: Academic.

———. 1987. "Opportunity Structure, Cultural Boundaries, and Literacy." In *Language, Literacy, Culture*, ed. Judith Langer, 149–177. Norwood, NJ: Ablex.

Ohmann, Richard. 1976. *English in America.* New York: Oxford University Press.

———. 1987. "Use Definite, Specific, Concrete Language." In *Politics of Letters*, 241–251. Middleton, CT: Wesleyan.

Ong, Walter J. [1975] 1987. "Literacy and Orality in Our Times." In *A Sourcebook for Basic Writing Teachers*, ed. Theresa Enos, 45–55. New York: Random House.

Phelps, Louise Weatherbee. 1988. *Composition as a Human Science.* New York: Oxford University Press.

Pratt, Mary Louise. 1991. "The Arts of the Contact Zone." *Profession* 91: 33–40.

Rodby, Judith. 1995. "(Con)Testing Ideas of Literacy (or There Are No Basics in This Class)." Unpublished manuscript.

———. 1996. "What It's for and What It's Worth? Revisions to Basic Writing Revisited." *College Composition and Communication* 47(1): 105–111.

Rose, Mike. 1985. "The Language of Exclusion." *College English* 47: 13–29.

———. 1989. *Lives on the Boundary.* New York: Penguin.

Rossman, Jack, et al. 1975. *Open Admissions at City University of New York.* Englewood Cliffs, NJ: Prentice Hall.

Rouse, John. 1979. "The Politics of Composition." *College English* 41(1): 1–12.

Royster, Jacqueline. 1990. "Perspectives on the Intellectual Tradition of Black Women Writers." In *The Right to Literacy*, ed. Andrea Lunsford, Helene Moglen, and James Slevin, 103–112. New York: Modern Language Association.

Russell, David R. 1992. *Writing in the Academic Disciplines: 1870–1990.* Carbondale, IL: Southern Illinois University Press.

Schultz, Lucille M. 1994. "Elaborating Our History: A Look at Mid-19th Century First Books of Composition." *College Composition and Communication* 45(1): 10–30.

Scribner, Sylvia, and Michael Cole. 1981. *The Psychology of Literacy.* Cambridge: Harvard University Press.

Shaughnessy, Mina. 1977. *Errors and Expectations.* New York: Oxford University Press.

Smith, Barbara Herrnstein. 1988. *Contingencies of Value.* Cambridge: Harvard University Press.

Smith, Frank. 1986. *Insult to Intelligence.* New York: Arbor House.

Smith, Thomas M. 1996. "Issues in Focus: Minorities in Higher Education." National Center for Educational Statistics. http://www.ed.gov/NCES/pubs/ce/c96007.html (August 4, 1996).

Smitherman, Geneva. 1995. "'The Blacker the Berry, the Sweeter the Juice': African American Student Writers and the National Assessment of Educational Progress." *ERIC Database.* Doc# ED366944. RIEJU94. (June 1995).

———. 1977. *Talkin' and Testifyin'.* Boston: Houghton Mifflin.

Steinberg, Stephen. 1974. *The Academic Melting Pot.* New York: McGraw-Hill.

Stepto, Robert. 1979. *From Behind the Veil.* Urbana, IL: University of Illinois Press.

Stewart, Donald. 1992. "Harvard's Influence on English Studies." *College Composition and Communication* 43(4): 455–471.

Stuckey, Elspeth. 1991. *The Violence of Literacy.* Portsmouth, NH: Boynton/Cook.

Taylor, Denny, and Catherine Dorsey-Gaines. 1988. *Growing up Literate.* Portsmouth, NH: Heinemann.

Trachsel, Mary. 1992. *Institutionalizing Literacy.* Carbondale, IL: Southern Illinois University Press.

Trimbur, John. 1991. "Literacy and the Discourse of Crisis." In *The Politics of Writing Instruction: Postsecondary*, eds. Richard Bullock and John Trimbur, 277–295. Portsmouth, NH: Boynton/Cook.

Veysey, Lawrence R. 1965. *The Emergence of the American University.* Chicago: University of Chicago Press.

Villaneuva, Victor. 1993. *Bootstraps: From an American Academic of Color.* Urbana, IL: National Council of Teachers of Education.

———. 1994. "On Writing Groups, Class, and Culture." In *Writing with*, eds. Sally Reagan, Tom Fox, and David Bleich, 123–140. Albany, NY: State University of Albany Press.

Vorhees, Lori. 1989. Listening with the Third Ear. MA Thesis, California State University, Chico.

Walker, David. [1848] 1969. *Appeal in Four Articles*. New York: Arno Press.

Wallace, Amy. 1995. "Figuring Out Who to Let in." *Los Angeles Times* (November 11): A1, A30.

Watkins, Evan. 1989. *Work Time*. Stanford, CA: Stanford University Press.

Webber, Thomas L. 1978. *Deep Like the Rivers*. New York: Norton.

Williams, Raymond. 1983. *Keywords*. New York: Oxford University Press.

———. 1961. *The Long Revolution*. New York: Columbia University Press.

Willis, Paul. 1977. *Learning to Labor*. New York: Columbia University Press.

Wolf, Thia. 1994. "Conflict as Opportunity in Collaborative in Radical Praxis." In *Writing with*, eds. Sally Reagan, Tom Fox, and David Bleich, 91–110. Albany, NY: State University of Albany Press.

Wolfram, Walt. 1969. *A Sociolinguistic Description of Detroit Negro Speech*. Arlington, VA: Center for Applied Linguistics.

Zeni, Jane, and Joan Krater Thomas. 1990. "Suburban African-American Basic Writing, Grades 7–12; A Text Analysis." *Journal of Basic Writing* 9(2) (Fall): 15–39.

Index